COOK LIKE A MAN

COOK LIKE A MAN

MASTER YOUR KITCHEN WITH 78 SIMPLE AND DELICIOUS RECIPES

FRITZ BRAND

Skyhorse Publishing

10 9 8 7 6 5 4 3

Library of Congress Cataloging-in-Publication Data is available on file.

Cover design by Laura Klynstra
Cover photo by Michael Le Grange
Food styling of cover photo by Caro Alberts

Recipe photographs by Fritz Brand, Claire Gunn
Food styling by Fritz Brand, Claire Gunn, Caro Alberts

Fritz Brand: www.fritzbrand.co.za
Claire Gunn: www.clairegunn.com
Caro Alberts: www.acalberts.co.za
Michael Le Grange: www.michaellegrange.com

Print ISBN: 978-1-63450-737-0
Ebook ISBN: 978-1-63450-738-7

Printed in China

Table of Contents

FOR MY MOTHER

I dedicate this book to my mother, Jessie, who sadly passed away during the writing of this book. She lived a life full of love, laughter, and compassion, and her memory will live on forever.

Introduction

This book goes out to the ones who don't know their sauté from their sous vide or their panna cotta from their *pomme purée*. The ones who like to tell themselves they can't cook. You see, I'd like to respectfully call bullshit on that.

I believe that if you can see, smell, taste, listen, and touch, there is no reason why you can't cook a perfectly acceptable meal. Get over your fear of failure, and get your ass in the kitchen. Every failure is nothing but an opportunity to learn from the mistakes you will naturally make along the way when learning any new skill. Try your best not to make the same mistakes over and over again, though—otherwise you are just being an idiot!

By nature, a recipe cannot include all the possible information one might need to cook a particular dish perfectly, in any given environment. There are, quite simply, too many variables involved in the process. Most recipes assume a certain base understanding or skill level of the cook.

This makes things difficult for beginner cooks who tend to cook recipes word for word, with little understanding of what's actually happening in the pan. Then, when a dish doesn't turn out as expected (as they tend to do), beginners have a hard time figuring out what went wrong.

I believe that once you learn the basic skills, techniques, knowledge, and lingo that gets thrown around in kitchens, you will find that the science and art of cooking is actually straightforward and very rewarding. In short, if cooking feels like a chore or a pain to you, you're doing it wrong.

To address some of the difficulties a beginner cook might face when starting out, I have included a lengthy introductory chapter called *Cooking 101* that will take you through the basics of cooking and give you a better understanding of how it all fits together. Hopefully, we can have some fun and avoid a few burnt offerings in the process.

Cooking 101

Cook Like a Man is not about making the fanciest version of anything. It's about getting people into kitchens to cook their own food, instead of relying on corporations that sell you ready-made meals with enough preservatives in them to make Keith Richards live another 250 years.

Cooking can be a rather frustrating affair—if you have no clue what you are doing. Learning the correct skills, techniques, and tools for the job will make your life a whole lot easier.

Just like trying to build a delicate dollhouse with a twelve-pound hammer, dicing an onion with a steak knife will cause you a considerable amount of frustration and could result in far too much money going into the swear jar. When I watch my friends cook and see them dicing an onion with a steak knife for five excruciating minutes, I have to really constrain myself from shouting, "What the @#*^@$ are you doing?!" If a job that is supposed to take at most one minute with a chef's knife turns into a five-minute ordeal of beady foreheads and furrowed brows, I can understand why people think cooking is hard work. All that inefficiency adds up, and you end up spending far too much time on a basic meal.

Truth be told, though, as with any other new hobby or sport you pick up, once you learn the basic skills, techniques, lingo, and tools for the job, cooking becomes a really rewarding experience—something you'll carry with you for the rest of your life.

FIRST THINGS FIRST

So, you are all excited and ready to get cooking. I get it. But before you jump right in, there are a couple of things you need to know in order to make your journey to culinary excellence a whole lot easier.

The French term *mise en place* roughly translates to *put in place*, and it refers to the setup that happens before the cooking.

You will notice that the professional chefs at work or on TV always have loads of small containers and sauce bottles within arm's reach around them. One minute it looks like all they've cooked is a steak in a pan, and the next moment that steak is on the plate with seasonal vegetables and mushrooms, drizzled with a beautiful pan sauce and garnished with freshly picked herbs that have appeared out of nowhere.

That's the magic of *mise en place*. If you take the time to prepare (wash, clean, trim, chop, slice, dice) *all* your ingredients before you start cooking and organize them in easily accessible containers, cooking becomes a breeze. Having to stop midway through poaching eggs because you forgot to make the hollandaise sauce and chop the chives is a surefire way to screw up some eggs.

BASIC KITCHEN GEAR

Just like any craftsman needs his tools, it is essential that you have the correct gear for various jobs in the kitchen. Don't worry if you can't afford to buy all of it at once; you'll build up a collection over time, and in most cases, you'll be able to make do with another "not-quite-perfect-but-will-get-the-job-done" piece of gear. Below are some of the basics that any kitchen needs, and my recipes will call for some of these items. Any additional, fancier gear required for a recipe will be listed under the "Extra Gear" section.

Knives

Knives are your most valuable tool in the kitchen, period. Learning to choose the right one for the job and how to keep them all in good shape is essential to safe and effective cooking.

Get yourself a decent chef's knife, paring knife, and a good bread knife to start out with. A good knife doesn't have to cost you the world. If you love knives (like I do), by all means get a couple of custom knives made up for you and pay top dollar for it (like I did); but in reality, a *much* cheaper version with a decent blade and solid plastic handle will do the job just fine. Check out the ones available at a restaurant supply store—if it's good enough for a line cook to use, it's good enough for you.

Most important, keep your knives super sharp. People tend to fear a sharp knife, but a dull knife is way more dangerous. A dull knife will require you to exert more force than should be required, and it also tends to slip off foods instead of cutting into them on contact. Those two things combined can easily lead to instantly shortened fingers, instead of neatly sliced tomatoes.

Knife maintenance is a two-step process—sharpening and honing.

Sharpening

Traditionally, sharpening was done on a wet stone or grinding wheel, but these days you get all sorts of handheld or countertop gadgets that will make the process a lot easier. Small amounts of metal are shaved or ground off the blade in order to remove the dull edge and form a new edge at the correct angle, depending on the type of knife.

Japanese knives are typically sharpened to 17 degrees, while most Western knives are ground to 20 degrees. A thinner edge is a sharper edge, but it is also more fragile and will require more maintenance. Pick your favorite, and learn to maintain it properly.

Knife purists may yell "Sacrilege!" at the thought of using these new-fangled gadgets; however, learning to sharpen knives properly in the traditional manner is no easy task and will take years to master. Not everyone has the time or inclination for that. (I tried hard and failed miserably; I bought all the gear, watched all the videos, but still couldn't get the desired results.)

In the end, a knife sharpened from a gadget is much better than a dull knife you've butchered on the wet stone while listening to tranquil Japanese music.

Honing

You know that metal rod that you often see chefs running up and down their knives in a flashy manner? That's a honing steel, and, contrary to popular belief, it does not actually sharpen knives. Instead, it "hones" or realigns the edge.

With use, the edge of a knife will suffer small imperfections—bumps and curls that will make it duller than it actually is. Honing realigns these imperfections with the edge of the blade so your blade performs as it should. Get in the habit of honing your blade before each use to keep it in shape.

Cutting boards

Whatever you do, never use glass cutting boards. They may look pretty and seem easy to clean ("hygienic" and all that) but they will dull the edge of your blades like you won't believe.

Your main choices are wood, plastic, and bamboo, and to be honest I think they all work just fine. The choice is really what suits your budget, style, and the job at hand. I suggest getting a few of different sizes and materials. You don't want to clean a huge cutting board to make a sandwich, but you also don't want to carve a turkey on what looks like its surfboard.

Last, whenever you use a cutting board, make sure it stays securely in place and doesn't wobble about. It's dangerous to use a knife on a board that is unstable, so make sure that it stays put by first laying down a damp dishcloth on your work surface and then placing the board on top of it. The damp cloth will make it stick to your work surface, giving you a solid base of operations, booya!

Pots and pans

It's important to use the right pot or pan for the job. Apart from the volume of food it will hold, there are a couple of things to consider. For example, think about the material it is made of. While a nonstick pan with a Teflon coating may be great for cooking a delicate piece of fish without risking it sticking to the pan, it is rather crap at getting a nice, dark crust on a piece of steak. Here are various options of cookware types and cookware materials.

Frying pans

Frying pans, skillets, sauté pans . . . which do you use when? Let's break it down.

Sauté pans have straight, vertical sides, resulting in a larger surface area of the pan being in contact with the heat source. They are great for shallow frying and making pan sauces. Ironically, sauté pans are not that great for sautéing in that flashy "toss food up in the air and hope they fall back in the pan" manner. Their heavier weight and straight sides make this difficult. However, you can still sauté in them by quickly stirring stuff around with a wooden spoon.

Skillets or frying pans have sides that flare or slope outwards, which makes it easier to do things like get a spatula under an egg prior to flipping it.

Ideally, you should have both shapes of pan. If not, don't fret; either will get the job done. Make sure you get one with an ovenproof handle so you can put it in the oven to bake things like frittatas, skillet cornbread, etc. Keep in mind that pan sizes are measured from lip to lip, not the cooking surface area, so a 12-inch sauté pan will fit more food than a 12-inch skillet.

Griddle pans

Griddle pans are normally made from cast iron and have raised lines or ridges across the surface of the pan. If you want to get those restaurant-style grill lines on a steak, this is your ticket.

Personally, I prefer my steak to have a dark brown crust all over (not just thin lines of it), so I don't use my griddle pan that often. Griddle pans are handy to have around, but I'd leave them lower down on the priority list as you build up your collection.

Saucepans

Saucepans are small pots with long handles, like the handle found on a pan. They are great for making sauces, boiling eggs and veggies, or forming part of a double-boiler. Saucepans are real workhorses in the kitchen, so get a couple of them in different sizes, with lids.

Dutch ovens

Dutch ovens are thick-sided, heavy-bottomed pots with a tight-fitting lid. Traditionally made from cast iron, but you also get them in cast aluminum, ceramics, glass, or steel. These days, the best Dutch ovens for kitchen use are made from enamel-coated cast iron, my favorite brand being Le Creuset. They are expensive, but if you take good care of them, your grandchildren will be cooking in them one day.

Dutch ovens are great on the stove top for making soups or stews, boiling veggies, and even cooking rice. They also work well for oven roasts or braises, where you'll first brown the meat on the stove top before transferring to the oven for low and slow cooking. These pots retain heat well, so they're also good for serving food in at the table, to keep food warmer for longer.

Stockpots

Stockpots are good for making huge pots of soup, boiling pasta, or, well, you know, making stocks. I have a 14-quart stainless steel, no-name brand model that I bought at a restaurant supply store that serves me well.

Stainless steel

Stainless steel cookware falls somewhere in the middle for me. It has some of the good properties of cast iron and is easier to clean, but it doesn't excel in anything specifically. I see it as general use cookware. When I'm lazy, I'll admit that I reach for the stainless steel (or nonstick) pan, as it cleans up easily.

Nonstick

While most people love nonstick pans, and for good reason, they do have drawbacks.

First, there are concerns with the chemicals used to make these pans that may get into your food, especially when used at high heat or when they start chipping. To combat this, make sure you buy a pan of decent quality from a reputable brand. You will pay a lot more, but you don't want to leave your health in the hands of an unknown brand that is trying to cut costs at every corner.

Second, don't ever use a nonstick pan for high heat cooking—you will damage the surface and run the risk of chemicals leaching into your food.

Last, when the coating starts to chip off, it's time to retire the pan. Some high-quality pans come with a guarantee. If the coating starts looking sketchy during that period, take it back to the store; with a little luck, they'll give you a new one.

Cast Iron

Cast iron has long been the vessel of choice for most things—your grandma used it daily, and it's friggin' awesome. It retains heat very well and can be used on any heat source (even straight on a fire). More important, it is great at developing that dark-brown crust on the surface of food, you know, that thing your taste buds love.

The main drawbacks of cast iron are that the pans are heavy and they require seasoning from time to time. For us lazy buggers, it is not dishwasher-safe. These drawbacks will not sway me, though. I love my cast iron pans. Once you get the hang of cooking and caring for these bad boys, you will know what I am talking about.

Best of all, they can be found at cheap prices at thrift stores and flea markets, though often looking rusty and worse for wear. With a little elbow grease or a wire brush attachment on a drill (wear gloves), you can get the rust off. Season it properly, and have yourself a friend for life.

Carbon Steel

These pans are popular in restaurant kitchens, and for good reason: they are absolute workhorses. Similar to cast iron in many ways, carbon steel retains heat well and is great for getting that perfect crust on fried foods, but it also requires seasoning and maintenance.

Carbon steel typically has a smoother surface and is much lighter than the cast iron pans of yore. They are my favorite pans to cook with when I feel like pulling out all the stops.

How to season cast iron or carbon steel pans

Cast iron and carbon steel pans need to be "seasoned" before use. No, this does not mean hitting it with salt and pepper (though salt can be used as an abrasive to clean the pan, but that's another matter). Seasoning refers the process of applying a thin layer of oil to the pan and heating it up for a period of time until the oil bonds to the metal.

As you heat up the oiled pan, a number of chemical reactions occur (I won't go into the details here), and a nonstick surface bonding is created. At first you'll see a couple of darkened blotches in the pan. As the seasoning builds up with use, it will darken and eventually become black. This discoloration is called a patina, and should be preserved, not scrubbed off after every use (unless you really enjoy seasoning your pans before every use).

To season a pan, preheat the oven to 450°F / 230°C and place a layer of tinfoil or a large baking tray on the bottom shelf to prevent oil from dripping onto the healing element. Give the pan a very thin coating of vegetable or canola oil, inside and out, then place it upside down in a preheated 450°F / 230°C for 30 minutes.

If you have a hood extractor, turn it on, and open the windows in your kitchen, as some smoke is bound to be generated during this process.

How to clean seasoned pans

Seasoned cast iron or carbon steel pans should not be cleaned in a dishwasher or with abrasive soaps or detergents. The best is to give it a light scrub under warm running water, then wipe it dry with a kitchen towel. For stuck-on food particles, use coarse or kosher salt under a kitchen towel to scrub it off, then rinse under running water and wipe clean.

Make sure no water remains in the pan after cleaning, as that can cause rust. The best way I've found is to put the pan on the stove and heat it up to high, until all the water has been removed, then apply a light layer of oil and allow the pan to cool. The removal of remaining water, together with the oil coating, will prevent rust from forming while the pan is not in use.

Surface area

You should always bear in mind that the surface area of a cooking vessel will have an impact on the way it cooks the food inside it. For example, if you want to reduce a sauce in a hurry, I'd suggest using a wide pan so more of the sauce gets exposed to heat on the bottom of the pan and more of the water in the sauce is able to evaporate.

On the other hand, when I make scrambled eggs and want to prevent the eggs from overcooking too quickly, I like to use a small saucepan so less of the egg is in direct contact with the heat, allowing for slower, gentler cooking.

Baking sheets and dishes

You need ovenproof baking dishes in various shapes and sizes for making casseroles, baking puddings, roasting vegetables, and, of course, making the almighty lasagna.

Baking sheets (or cookie sheets) are great for baking cookies (duh!), but they are also very handy for a variety of other tasks in the kitchen, from bulk-toasting bread to feed the hungry hordes to grilling pork chops. Get yourself a few in different sizes at a restaurant supply store; they don't have to be fancy.

Mixing bowls

Mixing bowls are one of those things you can't have too many of, and you want them in a variety of shapes and sizes.

Stainless steel ones are a good way to go, and please don't buy the fancy triple-coated versions with the nonskid bottoms, go to a catering supply store and buy their no-name brand stainless steel bowls, you should be able to pick up a small, medium, and large one for ten bucks, and that will get you started. Don't get me wrong: those thick, heavy bowls with the rubber pads on are nice, but they're not heatproof, so you can't use them as a double boiler (you'll learn about this later, don't worry).

Hand-held apparatuses

Spatulas

Spatulas are a bit of a weird one. People all over the world have different names for that thing we use to turn pancakes or eggs over. I grew up calling it an egg lifter, but I've later learned that the most widely used term is a spatula.

Apart from the egg turner–thingy, there are a whole bunch of other tools used for scraping food from the side of pots, folding cake mixtures, scooping things from curved bowls, etc., that are also called spatulas. You will eventually need a variety of them in order to have the best tool for the job at hand. Buy yourself a different kind of spatula every couple of months and build up a collection.

Whisks

Whisks are great for mixing and aerating wet ingredients. Get yourself a nice big wire whisk, as well as a smaller one for everyday use. A bigger whisk will make it easier to aerate mixtures, which is great for whipping cream or egg whites and maybe making mayonnaise.

The smaller one you can use to mix vinaigrettes, whisking eggs before making omelettes, etc., but to be honest you can get by with a fork for most of those tasks.

Spoons

Wooden spoons are by far my favorite stirring tool. They're great for scraping bits of food off the bottom of the pan during the deglazing process (see page 25), and they won't scratch your cookware. Just make sure you oil them every month or so with mineral oil so they don't dry out too much.

Apart from these, you also need a soup ladle or two and a slotted spoon to lift things out of water (like when making poached eggs).

Tongs

Yup, tongs are not just for grilling; they are also very handy in the kitchen. Again, you can buy these at a restaurant supply store. I have a couple of stainless steel tongs, as well as a rubber-coated one for when I am working with nonstick cookware.

They are great for turning things over in a pan and are just as awesome for serving pasta portions and generally handling hot ingredients that are large enough to be gripped with a tong.

Grater

Originally designed as a woodworking tool (until the housewives got wind of it), the grater is an incredible tool that you'll find in virtually all professional kitchens. I like to use the brand Microplane. The original model is a fine zester / grater that you'll just have to use in order to understand how awesome it is.

It makes quick work of zesting fruit and easily and efficiently grates chocolate, whole spices, garlic, and all sorts of other things. Once you've used it to grate some real Parmesan cheese over a bowl of pasta, you'll understand what I mean. Just get one, you won't be sorry.

Electronic scale

Electronic scales (instead of the ones your Grandma used) can make your life a hell-of-a-lot easier. They are easier to read, and most of them have a "tare" function. It sets the scale back to zero, ignoring the weight currently on top of it.

This allows you to add multiple ingredients to the same mixing bowl; just press the button after each ingredient and start weighing out the next one. It sounds simple, but it really can save you quite a bit of time and washing up afterwards.

Measuring spoons and cups

No, the teaspoon you use to stir your coffee in the morning is not an accurate measurement spoon, and I'd like to see you accurately measure a quarter of a teaspoon by eyeballing it. Sure, for most home cooking you can eyeball things without disastrous results, but when it comes to things like baking, there's not much margin for error.

When measuring flour in cups, don't scoop the flour up with the cup until it is full. The flour will pack together and you'll end up with a lot more than a standard cup in there. First fluff up the flour a bit in the container with a fork to get it aerated. Scoop up the flour with a spoon and fill the cup, then scrape the back of a knife over the rim of the cup to level it off.

Things on rolls

There are five kitchen essentials that come on carboard rolls of various sizes: cling wrap, aluminum foil, paper towels, parchment / baking paper, and kitchen towels.

Again, I like to buy these in bulk from a restaurant supply store. No need to pay for fancy brand named versions; catering grade cling wrap will do you just fine.

Kitchen towels

Much like mixing bowls, you can't have too many of these, either, and you're also better off buying them in bulk at a restaurant supply store. The ones at the supermarket are way overpriced.

I use kitchen towels for much more than just drying dishes. From keeping cutting boards and mixing bowls in place to handling hot stuff coming out the oven, having plenty of these around is never a bad thing. They tend to be a little like the socks of the kitchen, disappearing all the time, no matter how hard you try to keep things organized. Now I just buy them in bulk packs at a restaurant supply store. Some things are just not worth losing your mind over.

FATS AND OILS

Not all oils are equal, and unlike what you see on TV, olive oil is not the be-all and end-all of cooking. Sure, it is great, but there are instances where it is not the best oil for the task at hand. Knowing the characteristics of some other oils will allow you to choose the right fat for the job, resulting in a better dish and making you a better cook.

Olive oil

Olive oil is used in most forms of Italian cooking, as it imparts wonderful flavor, but it is not always the best option. When you are cooking delicate things like eggs or fish, using a strongly flavored olive oil might completely overpower the main ingredients, which is not a great idea. It also has a much lower smoking point than other fats, so it is not well suited to frying at high temperatures for extended periods of time, say, for example, when deep frying chicken.

Neutral oil

"Neutral" oils like canola or vegetable oil are great to use when you do not want to impart the flavor of the oils into the dish, as these are virtually flavorless. They often have a high enough smoke point to make frying at high heat possible. I like to use these with butter, so the dish benefits from both the flavor of the butter and the higher smoke point of the oil.

Coconut oil

Coconut oil has a nice flavor and a fairly high smoke point. I use it mainly in Asian-style dishes and stir fries.

Butter

Some time ago, scientists discovered that the saturated fat in butter is bad for us and proposed that we start eating their new invention, margarine. Most folks moved over to margarine and thought all would be well in the world forevermore.

Thankfully, recent studies have shown that their roles have reversed. Overly processed foods (like margarine) are the real enemy, while natural things (like butter) are good for us (Hallelujah!).

Regardless of which works better for you, butter is by far the best-*tasting* fat around, and most recipes can be improved by simply adding more butter. Most professional kitchens use *loads* of the stuff, and for good reason—it tastes like heaven. Want to know what makes the restaurant-down-the-road's mashed potatoes so awesome? Butter, and lots of it.

Clarified butter

Unsalted butter consists mainly of butterfat, water, and milk solids. Clarified butter is basically just butterfat with the water and milk solids removed. This increases its smoke point substantially, as the milk solids that usually burn easily are no longer present. This means you can fry foods in clarified butter at much higher temperatures, while still getting the great flavor only butter can provide.

Animal Fats

Using animal fats, like lard and tallow, for cooking can be a great way to add additional flavor to a dish. For example, if you cook a beef burger patty in beef tallow, you will add extra beefy flavor to the burger. As I've explained, it's all these little bits of things you do that really add up in the end, separating the men from the boys.

SEASONING

Confused with all the different kinds of salts out there? Let's have a look at the most common ones and learn about when to use which.

Chemically, there is very little difference between the various kinds of salts. They are all almost pure sodium chloride (NaCl), barring a touch of iodine, some anticaking agent, and a few additives here and there. The main difference among salts is in the size and hardness of the crystals.

Due to the differences in crystal size, you can't use volume-based measurements like cups and spoons interchangeably. A cup of table salt will be way saltier than a cup of Maldon sea salt, as the smaller crystal size of table salt allows fewer air pockets and enables you to pack a lot more salt into the cup.

Table salt

This is the stuff most people have in their homes—tiny crystals of similar size, as found in saltshakers all over the world. Table salt usually contains iodine (we apparently need trace amounts of iodine to develop properly), and an anticaking agent to make it flow better. Sea salt and other more natural, unprocessed salts will probably also bring along a few trace elements depending on where and how they were harvested, but, in the end, no one will be able to tell which type of salt you used in your tomato soup.

Table salt is often used with baking, as its small, uniform crystal size allows for more accurate volume-based measurements.

Kosher salt

Most chefs and serious cooks will likely use kosher salt for day-to-day tasks. Its medium-sized crystals make it easier to handle with your hands, and that is how most chefs season things—by feel. Try taking a pinch of kosher salt between your fingers, then try do the same with fine table salt, and you'll see what I mean.

Finishing salts

These are the fancy, expensive salts like Maldon and the like. Their larger crystal size makes for more contrast in a dish, where you will get bites with a burst of saltiness and some without, making the meal more interesting as your brain is entertained by the variations. These salts are added at the end of cooking and plating, right before serving the dish. You don't want the crystals to dissolve into the food, as that sort of defeats the purpose.

Herbs and Spices

Having a good arsenal of herbs and spices at your disposal opens up a world of opportunities when it comes to flavoring your food. The same basic ingredients (like chicken and vegetables, for example) can be turned into a variety of dishes by simply changing the herbs and spices used.

Modern society has grown accustomed to using ready-made spice mixes and just-add-water sauces, but I believe we are doing ourselves a disservice. Factory-made flavorings can never compare with a home-grown, made-to-measure creation that you've carefully adjusted over time to your liking.

Fresh herbs

I grow fresh herbs in a small four-by-four-foot patch outside my house. It's really cool to be able to go outside and snip a few leaves off as you need them, rather than buying a pack of herbs and only using a quarter of them before they wilt and turn into ridiculously expensive compost bin additions.

Growing your own herbs is really easy, and you don't need a lot of space at all. Take some photos of any potential grow space on your phone. It doesn't have to be soil space—you can grow herbs in pots, planters, or bags, no problem. Note roughly how much sun each spot gets a day, and head to the nearest nursery. Show them the spaces you have in mind (with a rough idea of the sun hours involved), and they'll be able to advise you on what to plant, and when, where, and how to take care of it. If your plant starts looking weird or sickly at any time, photograph the leaves (or snip off the weird-looking ones) and show them to the nursery for advice. You'll soon learn what to look out for and how to manage common problems.

Here are a couple of the herbs I grow; I've also listed what foods they go well with:

Basil
Tomatoes, strawberries, garlic
Chives
Eggs, cheese, fish
Oregano
Chicken, pasta dishes, tomatoes, fish
Parsley
Garlic, seafood
Rosemary
Lamb, roast potatoes, focaccia
Sage
Pork, pumpkin, veal
Thyme
Mushrooms, roast beef, carrots, roast potatoes

Dried herbs and spices

If you cannot grow herbs in your area (or you are just a lazy bugger), use dried herbs instead. One teaspoon of dried herbs will give you roughly the same amount of flavor as one tablespoon of fresh herbs.

Dried herbs and spices lose their potency over time, so it is important to store them in air-tight containers away from light, heat, and humidity (moisture). I store mine in small labeled glass jars with rubber gasket lids, neatly tucked in a drawer, away from the aforementioned enemies.

If you can, avoid buying spices at the supermarket. They are often not of the best quality and have spent far too long on the shelves or stored in a warehouse. Instead, find a specialty market or spice store in your area, and buy small amounts at a time. This is one of the few instances where buying in bulk is not a good idea, unless you have a heck of a lot of food to cook. Since spices lose their potency quickly, buying small amounts from a store with a decent turnover is a good idea. The fresher you keep your spices, the better.

Whole Spices

Whole spices last longer, so wherever you can, buy them whole and grind them down as needed. A mortar and pestle is the traditional way of grinding spices (and it can be a therapeutic experience), but most days I am far too lazy and just use an electric grinder. Cheap electric coffee grinders are perfect for grinding spices. Just dedicate one specifically for spice grinding, or you'll end up with some pretty weird-tasting coffee.

Some of the whole spices I keep around include:

Star anise
Cloves
Cinnamon sticks
Coriander seed
Paprika
Cumin
Turmeric
Mustard seed
Black pepper
Nutmeg
*Vanilla bean**
Cinnamon
Garlic powder
Onion powder

And here are some of the spices I keep around in ground form:

Paprika
Cumin
Turmeric
Cinnamon
Garlic powder
Onion powder

People who shy away from spices associate them with "spicy foods" that burn your mouth to smithereens. In reality, only a few spices carry the heat that causes a burning sensation; the rest are just a quick, easy, and healthy way of adding loads of flavor to your dish.

I urge you to experiment with spices and try out various combinations until you build up an idea of the flavors that work for you. Google is your friend—when I feel like trying out a new herb or spice I've never cooked with, I find myself Googling, "What goes well with . . . ?" You are bound to get new ideas to try in your cooking.

*NOTES ON REAL VANILLA BEANS:

To use a vanilla bean, split it in half lengthways with a paring knife, then scrape out the tiny seeds with the back of the knife. The empty pod left behind is called the husk. You can soak the husk in any liquid to infuse it with the vanilla flavor. Just remember to fish it out at some point. You can also add just the seeds; reserve the husks for your sugar pot, and you'll have glorious vanilla-flavored sugar for fancy cups of coffee. Alternatively, use 3 teaspoons of natural vanilla extract per pod specified in the recipe. Stay away from the synthetic "vanilla essence"—it often has a harsh chemical taste that can ruin a delicate dish.

Cook Like a Man!

First off, I'd like to state for the record that I have, up until the time of this writing, not had any professional culinary training. What follows in this book is nothing more than lessons learnt along the way. Some from screwing up badly, and others stolen directly from YouTube (but most from messing up big time). That leads me to point one.

BE BRAVE

You're never going to achieve anything extraordinary by staying in your comfort zone. To achieve greatness, one has to be willing to take a few tumbles. The trick is to know when to play it safe and when to swing for the fences.

You should have a few epic staple dishes, preferably ones you can make without looking at the recipe. These you use when you simply can't afford to mess up, like when that hot date comes over for dinner the first few times.

Leave your experimenting for an easier crowd, like your eager friends who will eat anything if it means they don't have to cook or pay for it.

BE PREPARED

That old adage "failing to plan is planning to fail" certainly holds stock in the kitchen (excuse the pun). Nothing will make the wheels come off a cooking session quicker than realizing you are missing a few key ingredients halfway through the ordeal.

Sure, it may seem like an awful lot of hassle to apply some brain to the task at hand before actually starting, but the ready-fire-aim approach rarely pays off in life, and even less so in the kitchen.

PAY YOUR DUES

When taking up any new activity, you have two options.

You can go in with your humility in check and be willing to learn from others, pay your dues by putting in the work and dedication needed to master any skill, and then start kicking ass and taking names.

Or you can be the guy who deems himself better than others simply by the size of his overinflated ego. Believing you are better than others is priority number one, is it not? I mean, who cares about actual skill level, or the fact that you have to invite yourself to most parties?

The reality is we should never stop learning. Life is full of valuable lessons if you are willing to look for them. There is a treasure trove on culinary information out there. Over the centuries, French guys in silly hats, Italian grandmothers with heat-seeking rolling pins, and their equivalent heroes and heroines in every other culture around the world have been cooking food and figuring out better ways of doing it long before hipsters started Instagramming food.

Yes, we should always try to put our own spin on things and leave our mark on the world, but know that some things should not be messed with, and not everything can be improved. The best advice I can give you is to learn some of the classic dishes in a cuisine you enjoy. Master the techniques required and try to isolate its flavors, textures, and visual aspects—basically, figure out what makes it tick. You will learn a lot about cooking this way, if you put in the time.

STOP OVERCOOKING THINGS

One of the biggest mistakes I see amateur cooks make is overcooking pretty much everything they touch. Dry steaks, soggy spaghetti, mushy and lifeless vegetables; the list goes on. I'm not sure what causes us to do this; it could be the paranoia surrounding food safety issues, but this crap has to stop.

I urge you to try and undercook things for a change. Chances are you might still overcook it a little bit, but you'll end up with a better-tasting dish. Food that is slightly underdone can still be saved by a few minutes more in the oven, but once you have passed the point of no return, there is nothing to be done.

It is important to realize that cooking doesn't stop the moment you take a pan off the heat or a roasting tray out of the oven. The residual heat in the cooking vessel, the food, and any surrounding liquid is still hot enough to continue the cooking process—and it will continue to do so for quite some time.

This is why you will sometimes see chefs chuck vegetables in ice water straight after blanching them for a few minutes in hot water. The idea here is to stop cooking the vegetables 70 percent of the way, then rapidly stop the cooking process by cooling down the vegetables as quickly as possible. When it is time to serve them, they are brought up to the desired temperature again without being turned to mush.

Texture is a very important part of the eating experience, and vegetables should really have a little crunch left to them, otherwise you might as well serve them as a puree. If you are used to eating mushy vegetables, vegetables with some life left in them might seem odd to you. Captain Comfort Zone might shout, "These vegetables are *raw*! DO NOT PROCEED!" However, pay him no mind, keep an open mind, and taste the difference objectively; you might be pleasantly surprised.

KNOW YOUR INGREDIENTS, AND HOW TO GET THE MOST OUT OF THEM

It's important to know the correct cooking and handling techniques to get the most out of your ingredients. Most steaks, for example, do well over high heat on a grill, turning frequently, but if I were to cook thick prime rib steaks on the bone, I would cook them over medium heat first so the intramuscular fat can render out (raw fat does not eat well), before giving it a nice crust over high heat just at the end.

It all depends what you're trying to achieve. Cheaper cuts of meat can be tough as old boots, but if you cook them low and slow for a couple of hours, you'll have some of the most flavorful meat on the animal, fall-off-the-bone tender, because low and slow cooking has broken down the connective tissue over time and turned that old boot into soft, luxurious, meaty heaven.

UNDERSTANDING TASTE AND FLAVOR

Taste is one of the five senses that humans can perceive. It is the sensation experienced when a substance is placed in the mouth and it reacts with the receptor cells located on the taste buds.

The basic five tastes we are able to detect can be categorized as salty, sour, sweet, bitter, and umami. *Umami* is a Japanese word that can be described as a meaty, savory taste.

The flavor of food is a combination of taste, smell, temperature, and texture—keep that in mind when creating your own dishes. It is very important to balance the flavor of a dish. Do this by tasting the dish while cooking and adding complementary or contrasting flavors as you go until it hits "the spot."

TASTE AND SEASON OFTEN

One of the best habits you can pick up is to taste your food often and adjust the seasoning as you go. You will also learn how the characteristics of food may change during the cooking process—for example, how tomatoes break down over cooking and become sweeter and richer.

Most people like to adjust seasoning at the end of cooking, just before serving, but I believe you'd be doing the ingredients a disservice. I believe that food should be correctly seasoned all the way through the cooking process to produce maximum flavor.

FOLLOW THE FAT

Most of the flavor-carrying molecules in meat are repelled by water, but they dissolve in fat. What this means is that when we cook meat, most of its flavor will be in the fat. That's why a rib-eye steak has way more flavor than a filet mignon, and why the filet usually gets served with a robust pan sauce to make up for the lack of flavor in the meat itself.

A pan sauce is made with those dark brown bits of residual meat that get stuck in the pan (called *sucs* in French). We'll just go right ahead and call it *meat candy*. Leaving that meat candy in the pan is one of the silliest things you can do as a cook. To the uninformed, it might look like you burned the pan again, but in reality, the meat candy left at the bottom of the pan is *loaded* with flavor, and it should be illegal to wash that stuff down the drain.

If you're cooking a lean piece of meat, you're already running low in the flavor department and cannot afford to let the most flavorful part of the meat be washed away in the dishwasher.

But then, how are you to remove it? Deglazing, of course . . . (see page 25).

KEEP IT SIMPLE

The majority of the more memorable dishes I've eaten in my life were also the simplest. There is a little bit of magic that happens when you take local and seasonal ingredients at their prime and put them in the hands of someone with the skills and knowledge to get the most out of each ingredient, as well as the confidence to let each stand on its own without being "assisted" with complex sauces or adornments.

To this day, my favorite way of eating potato is simply baked in its skin, served with butter and salt—nothing more.

Yes, there are times when you'll want to pull out all the stops and hit it out of the park, but for starters, keep things simple and focus on doing things right instead of doing lots of things badly. Before you know it, you'll be cooking kick-ass food without consulting recipe books.

GOOGLE IS YOUR FRIEND

We live in the information age and should learn to use that to our advantage. If you own a smartphone, you're basically walking around with the world's biggest library of information in your pocket. There is a wealth of knowledge out there, if you take the time to look for it. You're not the first guy trying to fry a piece of fish without it sticking to the pan! Type your troubles into Google, and a truckload of info will be thrown right back at you. Granted, not all of it might be legitimate, but you'll be able to pick up the root of the problem and figure out a solution by sifting through a couple of blog posts or YouTube videos.

Research dishes as much as you can, try out as many variations as you can. See what works for you and what doesn't, and ask lots of questions. Keep learning.

Essential Kitchen Techniques

Mastering the art of cooking can be a daunting affair, but don't fret, I've got your back. Once you understand the basic techniques, you will notice that a lot of the fancier recipes out there are just variations of the same thing. The technique stays the same; it's just a few ingredients that get changed.

Here are some of the basic techniques that you'll need to get a grip on in order to tackle more advanced recipes like it ain't no thang. I provide step-by-step instructions, along with a photo for each step, so you can track your progress as you go.

1

2

3

4

5

6

7

8

How to Make Mayonnaise

Making your own mayonnaise at home is quite a magical affair. Technically, oil and water do not mix, and since mayo mainly consists of oil and egg yolks (which are 50 percent water), it should not work, so what gives? The magic happens through the process of emulsion, permanently combining two liquids that normally do not mix.

You can temporarily combine oil- and water-based ingredients, for example, when making salad dressings by whisking them together like crazy, but if you let the mixture stand for a little while, you will see it split into two parts, with the oil at the bottom and the water-based ingredients on top.

Enter the humble egg. It contains an emulsifying agent called lecithin, which keeps things together once combined.

Give this a try, and you'll see how the volume and texture of the mixture changes the more oil you add. As a bonus, you will have a batch of delicious homemade mayonnaise at hand, which is far superior to the store-bought variety. At first, you might think it tastes weird, but that's just because you are used to the fake stuff. Once you get used to real homemade mayo, there is no going back.

EXTRA GEAR

Plastic squeeze bottle

INGREDIENTS

3 large egg yolks
2 tsp Dijon mustard
1 Tbsp white wine vinegar
3 cups neutral oil (like canola)
Salt
Cracked black pepper
2 Tbsp lemon juice

METHOD

1. Whisk the egg yolks, mustard, and vinegar together.

2. When the mixture becomes light and foamy, you can start adding the oil.

3. Add the oil *very slowly* while whisking like a demon. I like to use a plastic squeeze bottle for this to allow me to control the flow of oil. If you add too much oil too quickly, the mixture will split.

4. Once the mixture starts to thicken up, you can increase the amount of oil you add while whisking, but don't go overboard.

5. As you get close to using up all the oil, the mixture should be thick and creamy.

6. Add a pinch of salt and pepper, and keep whisking.

7. Add the lemon juice, and whisk through. This should thin out the mixture a little bit.

8. Taste and adjust seasoning as needed. And there you have it, your own homemade mayonnaise!

1

2

3

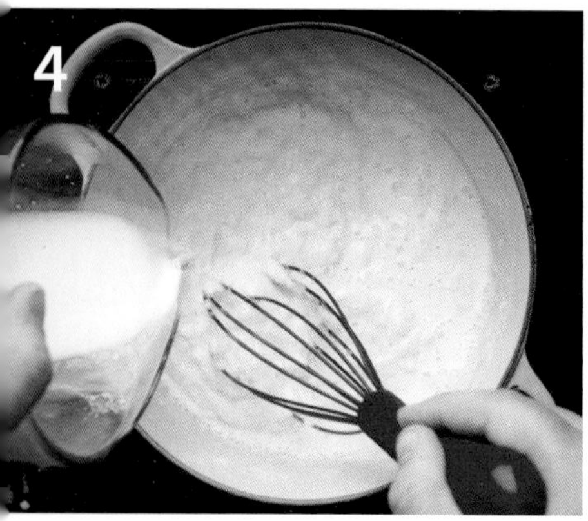
4

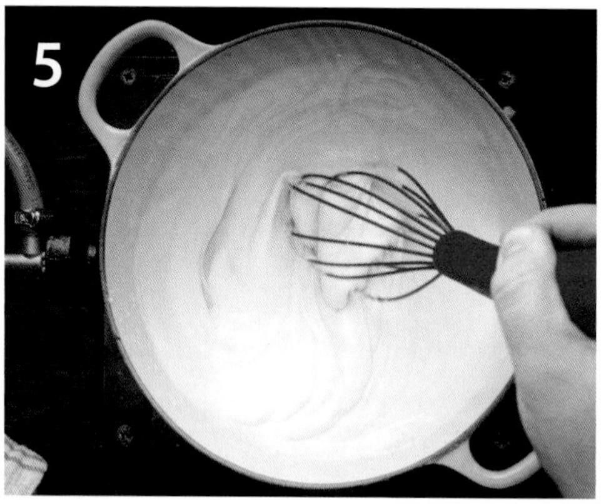
5

6

7

8

How to Make White Sauce

White sauce is a not so distant cousin of béchamel, one of the five French mother sauces. The original recipe involves an onion studded with cloves and whispering sweet nothings to the sauce as you whisk away.

White sauce is a slightly simplified version and is one of the most important sauces you should learn how to make. Once you have this technique down, you can easily make a whole host of sauces (think cheese, pepper, mushroom, mustard) by adding more ingredients to a white sauce base.

White sauce is also a big part of making a good lasagna, and we all love lasagna, right? Get this technique under your belt and you will never be too far away from a decent lasagna. That seems like a good enough reason to me.

INGREDIENTS

4 Tbsp butter
4 Tbsp flour
2 cups milk (heated to warm in the microwave)
Pinch nutmeg (freshly grated, if you can)
Salt
Cracked black pepper

METHOD

1. Place the pot on medium heat, and melt the butter while moving it around with the whisk.

2. Add the flour, and whisk into a paste.

3. Let the paste cook for 2–3 minutes while whisking. You don't want it to brown, just cook out the raw flour taste. If it starts to brown, go to step 4.

4. Add half the milk, and whisk like a demon into a smooth paste.

5. Add the rest of the milk, and whisk again.

6. Grate in a teeny bit of whole nutmeg with a grater, or pop in a pinch of ground nutmeg.

7. Turn down the heat, and let the mixture simmer for 5 minutes while whisking continuously so it doesn't catch on the bottom of the pan. Add a pinch of salt and pepper to taste.

8. Whisk through, and you are done!

1

2

3

4

5

6

7

8

How to Brown Meat Correctly

Many beginner cooks make the mistake of not browning meat properly. The deep-brown color comes from caramelization and the Maillard reaction, both of which dramatically increased the depth of flavor you get from the meat. These processes occur at higher temperatures, from 285°F / 140°C upwards. The main reason people struggle with achieving deep-brown color is the element of water.

Ingredients release water as they cook, and if you have too much water in the pan, the ingredients boil instead of frying. The boiling point of water is 212°F / 100°C, so ingredients cooked in water will never be able to color; the temperature is simply too low.

The avoid this issue, fry meat in smaller batches so you don't overcrowd the pan. The smaller amount of water that gets released, the quicker it can evaporate. When the water has evaporated, you are back to cooking the meat in oil and fat, which is what you need for high-temperature frying.

In this example, I fry some ground beef in a few tablespoons of olive oil.

METHOD

1. Heat up the oil. Add the meat in small amounts, breaking up larger chunks with a wooden spoon.

2. As you can see on the right side of the pot, quite a bit of water is released. You will hear a boiling sound, which sounds like frying but is not quite the same.

3. Most of the water has evaporated now, nearly ready for frying.

4. You will notice the sound change to a louder, more aggressive crackle. The water is getting out the way, and the temperature is increasing. You are on your way to flavor town.

5. At this point, all the water is gone and the temperature is high, so you need to stir more often to prevent burning.

6. The meat starts to brown quickly; it's nearly there.

7. Ta-da, properly browned meat. Turn off the heat and remove the meat from the pan to avoid further cooking.

8. Now you are stuck with what looks like a burnt pot. But no, my friend, that is not actually burning; it is caramelized meat residue, which is extremely flavorful. It's basically meat candy. Do not wash this pot and throw that deliciousness down the drain. Check out the next guide on deglazing (page 25), the process of removing that flavor from the bottom of the pot and incorporating it into your dish.

1

2

3

4

5

6

How to Deglaze a Pan

If you learn one thing from this book, it should be deglazing. This essential technique will take an average dish to new heights purely from the amount of flavor it adds to the dish.

Make this a part of your process with anything you cook, and you'll reap major rewards (and look like a pro in the process!).

METHOD

1. This is what a pan typically looks like after frying some meat.
2. While the pan is on heat, add about half a cup of liquid. Water works, but acidic ingredients like wine, vinegar, and lemon juice work a little better.
3. Most of the residue will come off easily, boiling loose from the surface.
4. Scrape the surface of the pot with a wooden spoon to loosen the more stubborn scraps.
5. The bits of residue will mostly dissolve into the water, leaving you with an extremely flavorful liquid.
6. You're done! You can now add the rest of the ingredients to the pan and continue cooking, secure in the comfort that you've just dramatically increased the flavor in your final dish. You can also make a pan sauce from this point. Add some shallots, vinegar, or what have you, then thicken it up with corn starch and milk. Making a white sauce with this flavorful liquid will give the sauce a deep flavor boost.

1
2
3
4
5
6
7
8
9
10

How to Make Anchovy Butter

Compound butters (butter with other delicious things added to it) are a great way to add a finishing touch to a dish. Here, I will show you how to make anchovy butter, which I love to serve on top of a good steak.

Go wild and come up with your own flavorings that will complement whatever you are cooking; the technique stays the same.

INGREDIENTS

Handful of fresh Italian flat leaf parsley, stalks removed
4 anchovy fillets, drained
1 stick of butter, cut into cubes and left to warm up to room temperature
1 lemon

METHOD

1. Lay out your ingredients on a cutting board or work surface.

2. Cut up the parsley in a mug with scissors, or chop it up with a chef's knife.

3. Chop up the anchovy fillets, nice and fine.

4. Add the parsley and anchovies to the bowl with the butter, and zest one lemon in there.

5. Mash it all up with a fork, making sure the ingredients are evenly distributed and combined with the butter.

6. Lay down some plastic wrap. Scoop the butter onto it to loosely resemble a log shape.

7. Roll over the cling film, and continue shaping the log with your hands.

8. Work as many air bubbles as you can out with your fingers, then pinch together the ends.

9. Holding the ends tightly, place the log down in front of you.

10. Roll it forward, applying pressure downward as you go. Repeat steps 9 and 10 a few times until you have a nice, tight butter "sausage." Tie the ends or fold them underneath the butter, and place in the fridge to firm up.

1

2

3

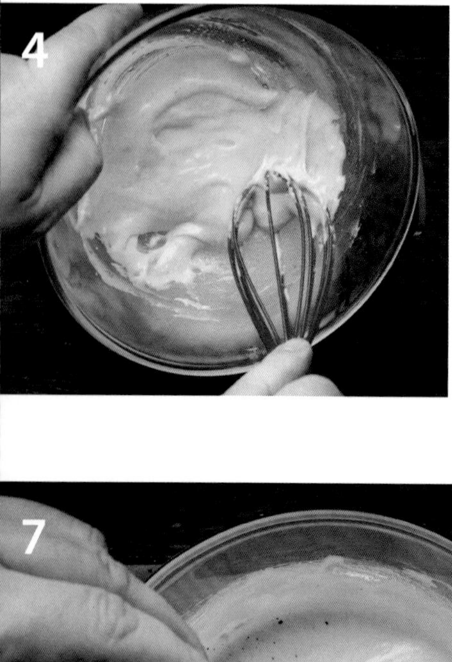
4

5

6

7

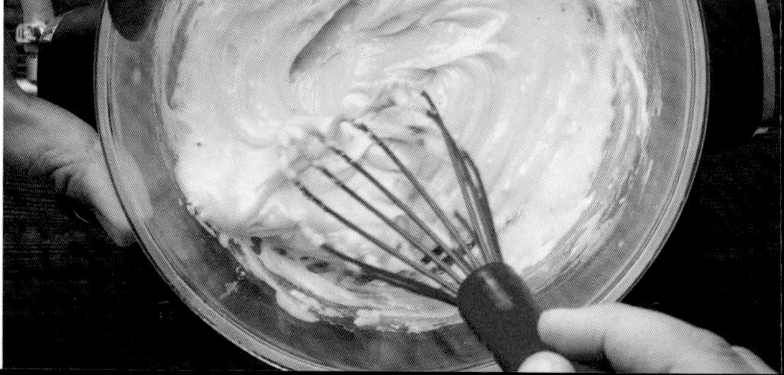
8

How to Make Hollandaise Sauce

Give me a poached egg on toasted sourdough, a few spears of grilled asparagus, and an indecent amount of hollandaise—and I am in brunch heaven.

Here's how you make it. The trick is to keep whisking the entire time, and manage the temperature. If you cook the eggs too fast, they will scramble, and we want none of that.

Making the sauce in a double boiler will help keep the temperature low and steady. To make a double boiler, fill a small saucepan about ¼ of the way with water and bring it to a slow simmer. Pop a metal or glass mixing bowl on top of the saucepan. You want the two to fit snugly, and the water in the saucepan should *not* touch the bottom of the mixing bowl.

Since water turns into steam at 212°F / 100°C, the contents of the mixing bowl will not exceed that temperature, and the steam buildup around the bowl will transfer the heat gently and steadily, with no hot spots like you would get if cooking directly on a heat source.

Remove the bowl from the pot from time to time to cool things off (keep whisking), and top up the water in the saucepan if it is starting to run low.

INGREDIENTS

3 eggs
1 tsp white wine vinegar
14 Tbsp (7 oz) butter, melted (skim the foam that accumulates on the top off with a spoon)
Squeeze of lemon juice
Salt
Cracked black pepper

METHOD

1. Fill a small pot with an inch or two of water, and bring to a gentle simmer.
2. Separate the egg yolks from the whites (see page 37). Add the three egg yolks and vinegar to a bowl that will sit snugly on top of the pot, and whisk until foamy. The bottom of the bowl should not be able to touch the water.
3. Slowly add in the butter, bit by bit, and whisk like mad until incorporated.
4. Lift the bowl from the pot every now and then so you don't build up too much heat.
5. Keep adding butter in small streams while whisking like your life depends on it, until all the butter has been incorporated.
6. Add a squeeze of lemon juice. This will thin the mixture out slightly and give it a nice lemony tang.
7. Add a pinch of salt and pepper, whisk through, and have a taste. Add more salt, pepper, or lemon juice as needed.
8. Whisk through to combine, and enjoy!

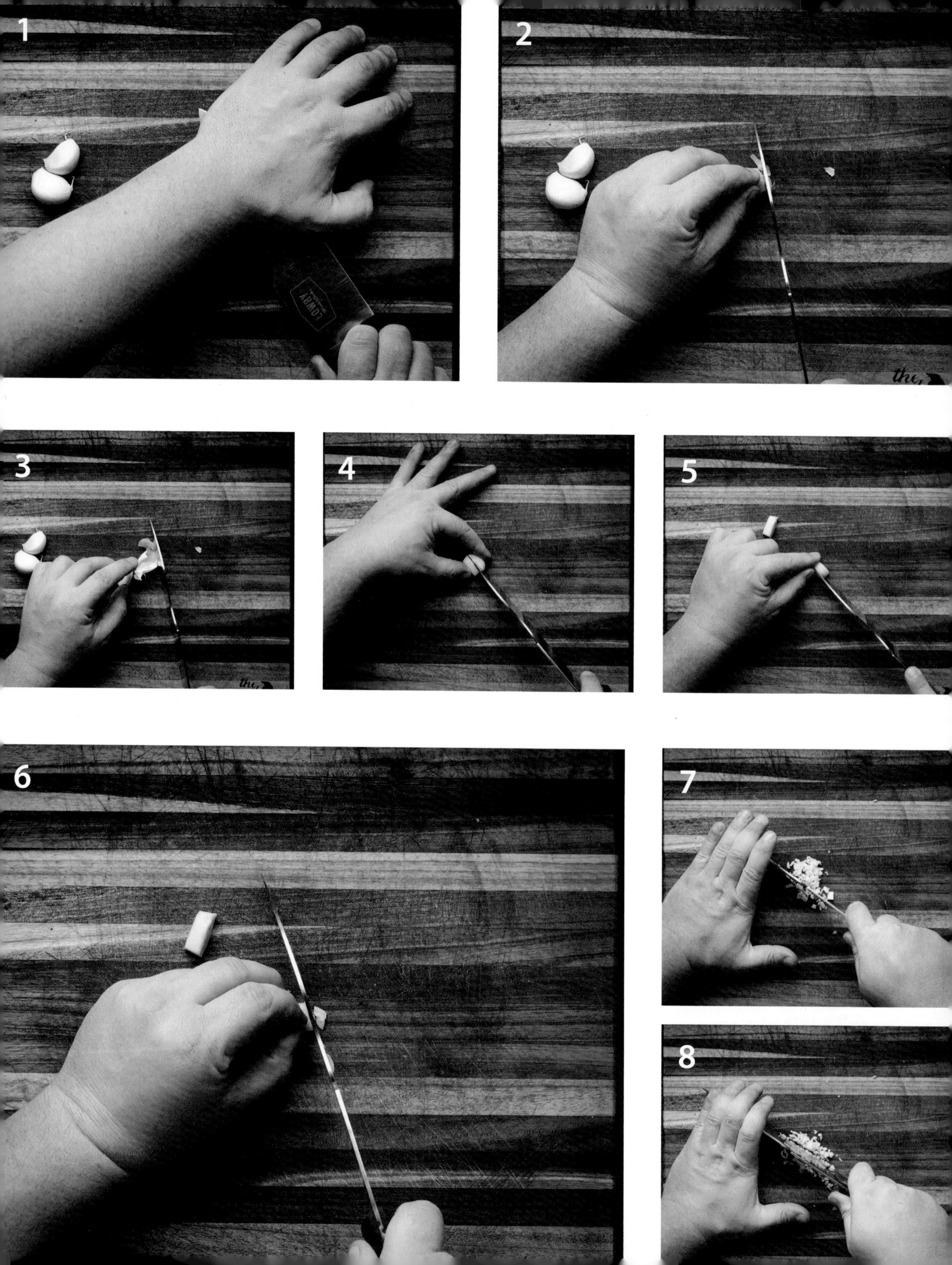
1
2
3
4
5
6
7
8

How to Peel and Chop Garlic

Working with fresh garlic is so much better than the crushed stuff you can buy at the store. Peeling garlic can be difficult, but I have a trick that will make it way easier.

Garlic can be prepared in various cuts, depending on the amount of garlic flavor you are looking for. The finer you chop garlic, the more pungent the flavor will be. You can slice thin slivers of garlic and fry them in oil for a simple pasta, or grind it down to a paste for a punchy stir-fry.

The technique below will allow you to peel whole cloves of garlic, which is essential if you want garlic slices. When I am in a hurry, I bash down the blade quite hard, squashing the clove. It's even easier to peel then, and a quick rough chop is all that is required.

METHOD

1. Place a clove of garlic on a cutting board, then push down on it using the flat side of a chef's knife until you hear a cracking sound.
2. Slice off the hard bits at both ends of the clove.
3. If you cracked the clove well, the peel (or most of it, anyway) will come right off when you slice off the ends. Remove any remaining peel with your fingers.
4. Slice the clove in half lengthwise. This will allow it to lay flat on the cutting board, instead of rolling around on its curved side, which could be detrimental to your fingertips.
5. Lay each half flat-side-down and make a number of small cuts lengthwise, almost all the way to the tip.
6. Now turn your knife sideways, and slice off the pieces.
7. After you've sliced both halves, hold down the pointy end of your knife with your left hand (keep your thumb safely out of the way), and with your right hand make a rocking motion over the chopped garlic, moving the blade as you go.
8. Scrape off the bits of garlic that stick to your knife, and continue chopping with that rocking motion until the garlic is as finely chopped as you want it.

NOTES:
If you'd like to make garlic paste, add a pinch of salt to the chopped garlic, and, using the flat of the blade, scrape the garlic and salt mix a few times across the board.

1
2
3
4
5
6
7
8

How to Dice an Onion

Learning how to chop an onion quickly and efficiently was one of the greatest discoveries of my cooking journey. Before that, it used to take me ages to peel and chop an onion, using a steak knife or whatever else I could find. The quicker and more efficiently you work in the kitchen, the more enjoyable it becomes. All the small bits of time and effort spared really do add up in the end.

With practice, this becomes so easy and simple that you'll wonder why you ever did it another way.

METHOD

1. Slice the onion in half lengthwise. You see that hard, stringy bit under my knife? That is the root. We want to keep the root attached to each half; it helps keeps things together.
2. Slice off the end that is opposite the root for both halves.
3. Peel off the skin by pulling with your fingers.
4. Now for some knife safety. Place your fingers on top of the onion as shown, fingertips exposed.
5. Move your knuckles forward without repositioning your fingertips. You see how your fingertips are now "hidden"? When slicing, you want the blade to move against your knuckles, with your fingertips safely tucked away. This will feel awkward at first, but so will accidently chopping off a fingertip, so take your time and get comfortable with this move; it will become second nature soon enough.
6. Make evenly spaced cuts across the onion, almost all the way to the root.
7. Turn the onion sideways and slice off the thin sections. Watch your fingertips. That's all there is to it. At first, this method will probably take you longer than your current method, and it might feel awkward. But trust me, once you get the hang of this, you will never go back.

1

2

3

4

5

6

7

8

How to Poach Eggs

I won't lie: poaching eggs can be a bit tricky. The main thing is you'll want to use the freshest eggs you can get your hands on. As eggs age, the whites become a lot runnier and looser, which makes it hard to get a properly shaped poached egg.

You also don't want the water temperature too high, as a full rolling boil will break the egg apart before it has time to set, and you'll end up with a mess. Keep the temperature just barely simmering, or even a bit lower than that, and you'll have a much higher chance of success.

As with anything, it takes a couple of tries to get the hang of it. Be brave and push on, and it'll be worth it. Poached eggs with hollandaise sauce is something you simply have to learn how to make.

METHOD

1. Fill a pot with about 4 inches of water, and bring it up to a very gentle simmer. Add a splash of white wine vinegar to the water.
2. Crack the egg into a small bowl or cup.
3. Gently swirl the water around with a spoon to make a whirlpool.
4. Gently lower the bowl into the middle of the whirlpool, and tip out the egg.
5. Leave the egg alone for 30 seconds to firm up a little.
6. Gently lift the egg from the bottom of the pot with a slotted spoon if required; you don't want it exposed to the higher heat on the bottom of the pot for too long.
7. After about 3–4 minutes after "drop time," the egg will be cooked. Lift it out of the water with a slotted spoon. Adjust this timing depending on how soft you want the egg to be.
8. Trim off any frilly bits with a pair of scissors. There you have it. Enjoy!

1
2
3
4
5
6

How to Separate Eggs

Separating eggs is pretty straightforward; nevertheless, I've had plenty of dudes asking me about my technique, so here is how I do it.

If you plan on keeping the egg whites to whip up a meringue later, you will need to make sure that you are using a very clean bowl and that no broken egg yolk mixes in with the whites. Egg yolks contain fat, and even a small amount will prevent the foam from forming when you whip the egg whites.

To that purpose, use two bowls, keeping a separate bowl on the side, and only transfer the whites from each egg to it once you are sure no yolk has gotten in there. It often happens that an egg yolk will break if you crack the egg too hard, and if you were separating all the eggs over one bowl, those whites would have been ruined.

METHOD

1. Gently, crack the egg on a flat surface to create a little crack in the shell, with most of the egg intact. You want to crack the egg on a flat surface rather than the edge of a bowl. If you crack too hard on the edge of a bowl, the edge will push up into the egg, taking shells with it and potentially breaking the yolk.

2. Hold the egg over the bigger bowl and carefully widen the crack with your thumbs to break the egg into two halves. Let the yolk fall into one of the halves, and keep it upright. Most of the whites will have dropped into the bowl.

3. To separate the yolk from the remaining whites, transfer the yolk to the empty half shell, allowing the whites to slide out of the shell and into the bowl. If you don't get this the first time around, transfer the yolk a few more times from one shell to the other.

4. Sometimes the egg whites can be stubborn and will stick to the side of the shell. You can scrape them loose with the cracked edge of an egg shell. If any broken bits of shell fall into the whites, remove by scooping them up with half an egg shell—much easier that trying to get the slippery buggers with your fingers.

5. Pop the separated yolk into the smaller bowl.

6. Repeat the process for however many eggs you've got, and remember to keep the whites free from egg yolks or any other fat, if you plan on using them later.

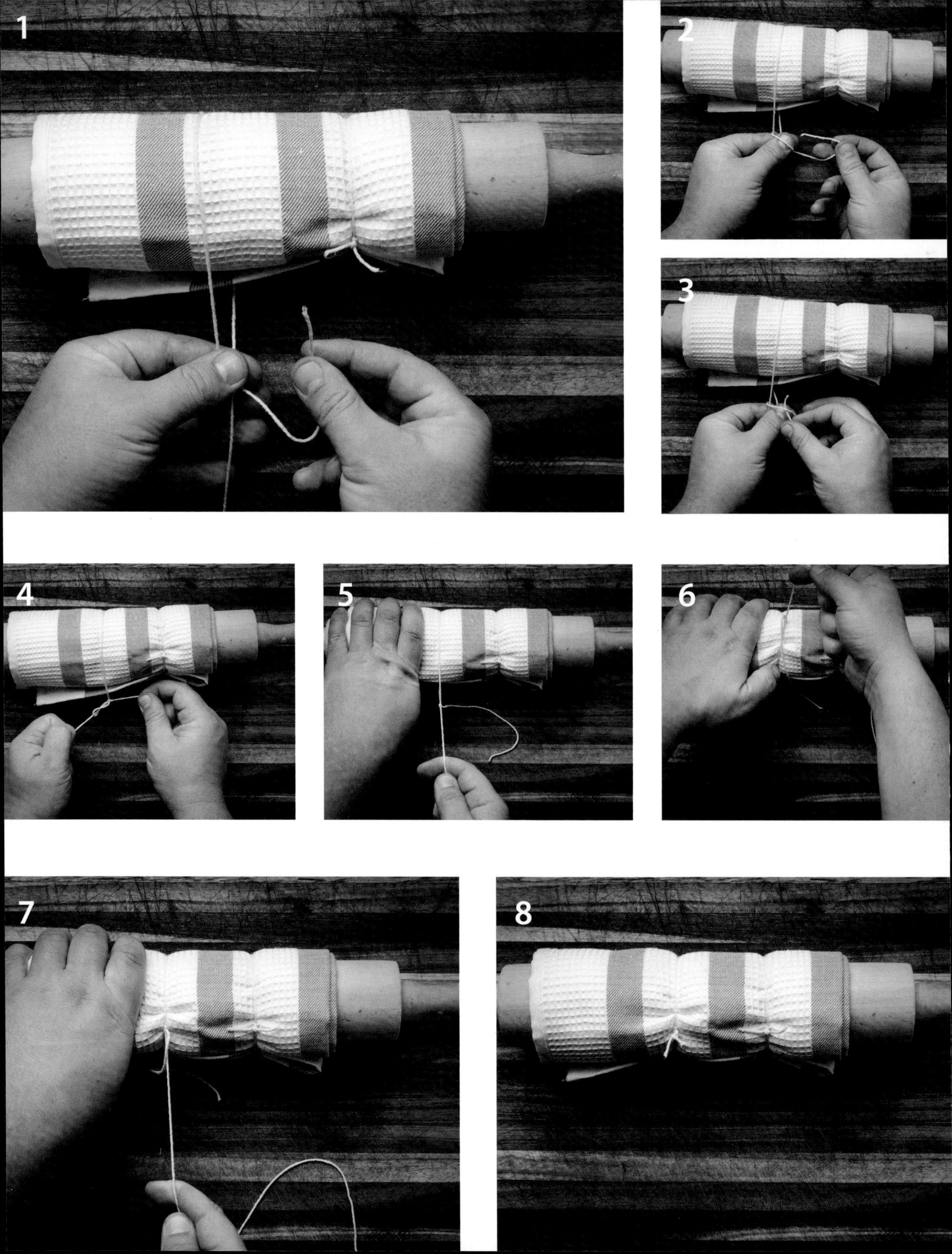

1
2
3
4
5
6
7
8

How to Tie a Butcher's Knot

If you're a meat-eating man like me, you owe it to yourself to learn how to tie a proper butcher's knot. It's perfect for tying up roasts or boneless rib-eye steaks for the grill to help them keep their shape. Unlike a regular shoelace-style knot, this is a slip knot, so you can tighten it as much as you want after the knot is set by pulling down on the string.

You can practice on a rolled-up towel, or a rolling pin with a dish towel wrapped over it, as I am doing here.

METHOD

1. Slide the cut end of the twine under the "roast" while holding the other end tight with your other hand. Throw the cut end back over, and pinch the two strings in your left hand, between your thumb and forefinger.
2. With your right hand, loop the cut end over and under your thumb and both strings.
3. Push the cut end down through the loop.
4. Pull both strings to set the knot.
5. Now, hold the roast with your left hand and pull the long end up toward you, just enough to tighten the string.
6. While keeping the string tight, pull the long end up toward the roast, pulling upward as you go. You will notice the string tightening around the roast, but there should still be a gap.
7. Pull the long end down firmly. The string will tighten more around the roast, and you should be all set. Try to keep all the knots in line with each other; it just looks better that way. Snip off the excess twine, and repeat as necessary.

Brunch

cm

Croque Monsieur SERVES 1

As far as grilled cheese sandwiches go, the croque monsieur is king. Toasted buttery bread, smoked ham and cheese smothered in creamy béchamel (white sauce), with crispy, grilled cheese on top. I mean, really. Trouble is, it can be a bit of a chore to make, as it takes time and effort to make a good béchamel.

My solution is to always make a cup or two extra whenever I make a batch of béchamel. That way, I have some ready to go whenever I start Craving the Croque.

INGREDIENTS

2 slices of bread, preferably sourdough
1 Tbsp butter
½ cup of white sauce (see page 21)
2 slices smoked ham
Cheddar cheese, grated
Salt
Cracked black pepper

NOTES:
Make your béchamel (white sauce) in advance; it keeps in the fridge for a couple of days.

Mix it up and try some different cheeses, hams, and types of bread until you have created your ultimate sandwich.

PREP

1. Preheat the oven to 350°F / 180°C.
2. If you are using soft white bread, toast it first so it can hold the weight of the sauce. Sourdough or other sturdier bread can be used as is.

METHOD

3. Spread a slice of bread with butter, and pop it on a baking tray lined with baking paper, butter side down.
4. Spread a layer of white sauce on the bread, then add the ham and grated cheese. Spread some white sauce on another slice of bread, and place it sauce-down on top of the sandwich.
5. Spread some more butter on top of the sandwich, then add another layer of white sauce and top with more cheese.
6. Switch on the broiler, and cook until browned on top. Season with salt and pepper.

Peanut Butter & Caramelized Banana Smoothie SERVES 4

I must admit, I'm not really a smoothie kind of guy. Give me bacon and eggs any day. I think it has to do with being allergic to most fruits as a child. I grew up thinking fruits were the devil, and not much has changed since then.

That said, I am not getting any younger, and I realize I should probably start getting healthier stuff down my gullet.

My girlfriend has taken it upon herself to come up with recipes that are deceptively healthy. That is, they sound amazing, they look amazing, and they even taste amazing; yet somehow they are packed with good things that the body needs. Guilt-free goodness and all that.

This is one of my favorite recipes—it's almost like a milkshake, I tell ya! Yeah, I know it's not *all* that healthy, really, but baby steps, okay!

EXTRA GEAR

Stand or stick blender

INGREDIENTS

3 bananas
3 Tbsp honey
2 cups full cream plain or vanilla yogurt
½ tsp cinnamon
2 heaped Tbsp peanut butter
¼–½ cup milk
3 blocks of ice
Salt

PREP

1. Peel the bananas, and slice them open lengthways.

METHOD

2. Add honey to a medium-sized pan, and place it on medium heat. Once the honey starts to bubble, put the bananas in the pan and let them caramelize with the honey. After about 5 minutes, they should be done. Remove from heat and set aside to cool.

3. Add all the other ingredients to a blender, and start blitzing. If it is not blending yet, add a little more milk. Once you have a good vortex going inside the blender, add the caramelized bananas and honey from the pan, and blitz. (You may need to heat the pan up again to loosen its contents.)

4. Last, add the three blocks of ice, and blitz those, as well. That's all there is to it.

Egg & Soldiers SERVES 2

Egg and soldiers is a classic British breakfast dish. The idea is that the thin pieces of toast in a row somehow resemble soldiers, and that the gentlemanly thing to do with said soldiers is to dunk their heads in eggs before biting them off.

Weird as this may seem, it's still delicious, and that sort of overrules the "who came up with *that* idea?" question.

EXTRA GEAR

Bread toaster
Stopwatch or timer (your phone should have one)
4 egg cups

INGREDIENTS

4 eggs
4 slices of white bread
Butter
Salt
Cracked black pepper

NOTES:
If you are serving these to children, go easy on the salt and pepper. In my experience, kids are more sensitive to strong seasoning and spices with heat.

METHOD

1. Place the eggs in the pot, and cover with about an inch of water. Put the pot on high heat. Place the first two slices of bread in the toaster. Keep an eye on the water. The moment it starts to boil, start your timer for 3 minutes, and lower the heat a little so you get a gentle, rolling boil.

2. Toast the other two slices of bread, and butter them all. Slice the bread into strips that are thin enough to dip into the egg—about ¾-inch thick should do.

3. After exactly 3 minutes, remove the pot from the heat. Fish the eggs out with a slotted spoon, and pop them on a folded-up dishcloth.

4. Place the eggs in the egg cups, and tap them gently on the side with a knife to crack, then cut through.

FINAL TOUCHES

5. Season the inside of the eggs with a little salt and pepper. Dip the soldiers in the eggs and chomp on! Then, dig in with a teaspoon to scoop out the rest of the egg, adding a little more seasoning if needed.

Chorizo & Tomato Baked Eggs SERVES 4

This dish hits the spot on so many levels, there's no wonder it's a firm favorite in countries the world over. Mexican huevos rancheros, Middle-Eastern and North-African shakshouka, Turkish menemen—they are all variations of the same thing: eggs cooked in a rich, spicy, tomato-based sauce.

It also works great as a hangover cure breakfast (or lunch if it was a *really* late night out). You can cook the chorizo and tomato sauce a day or two before and leave it in the fridge. Once that step is done, all you have to do in the morning is pour the sauce in a pan, heat it up, pop in the eggs, and let it bake in the oven for about 15 to 20 minutes. Sorted.

INGREDIENTS

1 white onion
4 inches of spicy chorizo
8 slices ciabatta bread
1 Tbsp olive oil
1 tsp salt, plus extra to season
1 14-oz tin chopped tomatoes
1 generous pinch of sugar
1 tsp mixed Italian dried herbs
1 handful grated Parmesan or other hard cheese
4 eggs
1 pinch cracked black pepper
Chives, to garnish (optional)

PREP

1. Preheat the oven to 350°F / 180°C.

2. Chop the onion into chunky pieces and set aside. Slice the chorizo in discs and set aside.

METHOD

3. Slice your ciabatta as thick as you'd like it. Heat up some olive oil in a pan, and swirl the slices of bread around in the pan to coat them evenly. Fry the slices of bread until golden and crispy on both sides. Sprinkle with salt to season, and set aside.

4. Put an ovenproof pan on the stove over medium heat. Add a bit of olive oil, and fry the chorizo slices until crispy on the edges. Remove the chorizo from the pan, and set aside. Leave the flavored oil in the pan, though; that's good stuff right there.

5. Fry the onions until soft and golden. Add the tomatoes, salt, sugar, and mixed herbs to the pan, and give it a good stir. Turn down the heat, and simmer for 5 minutes. Add the chorizo, and stir through.

6. Make four small "indentations" in the pan of tomato sauce with a spoon, and grate some Parmesan cheese over the top. Break the eggs one at a time into a small bowl, and then gently tip it out into each "dam." You shouldn't take your time doing this, as the first egg you drop in will start cooking, and you want them to cook as evenly as possible.

7. Grate more Parmesan cheese over the top, and get that guy in the oven. Check in after 10 minutes. Here is where things depend on how you like your eggs.

8. If you want them runny enough so you are able to dip ciabatta in the egg yolks (as you should, just saying), then cook them for another 3–5 minutes, i.e., 15 minutes cooking time in total. If you want your eggs harder, 15–20 minutes in total cooking time would be the ticket. Ovens do vary, though, so adjust the timing to suit yours.

FINAL TOUCHES

9. Remove the pan from the oven, and sprinkle the eggs with salt and black pepper.

10. Garnish with fresh chives if you feel like being fancy.

Scrambled Egg on Toast SERVES 1

Making scrambled eggs might seem like a ridiculous recipe to put in a book, as it seems like such an easy thing to do. However, judging by the amount of times I've been served dried-up, rubbery eggs, I think it might be worth documenting a better way of going about it. Some of the best meals I've ever had consisted of the simplest food, cooked to perfection. Mastering this recipe will go a long way in showing you how cooking basic food correctly can transform the most ordinary of dishes into something extraordinary.

The danger with eggs is that they overcook in seconds. If you cook them to your liking and leave them in the pan while you butter the toast before dishing up, the residual heat left in the pan will overcook them.

To counter this problem, you need to do two things. First off, prep everything in advance. Don't put the eggs in the pan until everything else is ready. The toast should be ready; the plates, cutlery, and condiments should be on the table; and the coffee should be made. If you are cooking for guests, start ushering them to the table. When it comes to eggs, every second counts. In short, don't start cooking the eggs until the very last minute.

Second, you need to get the eggs out of the pan while they are still slightly underdone. It might feel weird to stop cooking eggs that are a little bit runny, but even if you dish up immediately, the residual heat left in the eggs will be enough to cook them the last bit of the way. Err on the side of going underdone—you can still fix that.

It is a fine line to keep. Ten seconds this way or that way, and you've missed the mark. Don't fret: once you get the hang of it, you will never have to eat rubbery, lifeless eggs again.

NOTES:

This recipe can easily be scaled up to serve more people if you have guests over for brunch.

I could try and give you exact times and all sorts of crazy rules to follow, but the reality is you will only learn to accurately gauge doneness by repeatedly cooking scrambled eggs, missing the mark a few times, and learning from your mistakes. My advice is to take them off the heat sooner rather than later.

INGREDIENTS

- 2 slices sourdough bread (or bread of your choice)
- 3 eggs
- 1 big knob of butter
- Salt
- Cracked black pepper
- Chives, to garnish (optional)

PREP

1. Toast the bread.

2. Crack the eggs into a small bowl, so they are ready to go.

METHOD

3. A pan of any size can work, but I like to cook scrambled eggs in a small saucepan. The small surface area at the bottom of the pan means a smaller amount of the eggs are in direct contact with the heat, slowing down the cooking process and making it easier to hit the sweet spot in terms of doneness.

4. I usually skip the step of buttering the bread and, rather, chuck all the butter in the pan with the eggs. This keeps the bread from going soggy while you cook the eggs; it means less work for you; and it also helps with the flavor and consistency of the eggs—a win-win-win situation.

5. To the actual cooking. Put your saucepan on medium-low heat, and add the butter. When the butter just stops foaming, drop in the eggs, and leave them alone for 2 minutes. Remove the pan from the heat, and start scrambling up the eggs with a wooden spoon, stirring continuously. You will notice that even while the pan is off the heat, the eggs continue to cook as you keep stirring. That's residual heat at work.

6. If you think the eggs are still way too runny, put the pan back on the heat for 15 seconds at a time, stirring continuously. You need to decide at what point to make the call that the eggs are ready.

7. At this stage, add the salt, and start moving toward the table. You want to serve the eggs while they are still runny—you should be able to pour them onto the toast by tilting the saucepan (be careful not to let it turn into a messy affair). If they are not pourable, they are already overcooked, and you should remove them from the heat a few seconds earlier next time.

FINAL TOUCHES

8. Once the eggs are on the toast, sprinkle salt on top and some pepper if you wish.

9. Chives also go really well with eggs. If you have some in the fridge or garden, snip a little over the top with scissors, and dig in!

Eggs Bacon-dict SERVES 2

I always thought that Eggs Benedict was quite difficult to make and only achievable in a restaurant kitchen by a brigade of dudes wearing floppy white hats. Truth be told, it's way easier than you think. You don't need any special equipment or fancy ingredients—and it can be made in 30 minutes flat.

Poaching eggs and whisking Hollandaise does require a bit of focus and practice, but just like riding a bike—once you get the hang of it, you are set for life. Let's get cracking.

NOTES:
You will have the chance to use a couple of basic techniques in this recipe: separating egg yolks (page 37), making Hollandaise sauce (page 29), poaching eggs (page 35), and making herbed paprika salt (page 248).

INGREDIENTS

2 large handfuls baby spinach
1 pack streaky bacon
2 English muffins
Hollandaise sauce (using two egg yolks, see page 29)
4 eggs
2 Tbsp olive oil
Herbed paprika salt (see page 248)

PREP

1. Preheat oven to 350°F /180°C.
2. Wash the spinach, and trim the stalks.

METHOD

3. Lay the rashers of bacon out on a baking sheet, and bake for about 15–20 minutes, depending on how crispy you want them.Slice the English muffins in half. Fry them face down in olive oil in a frying pan on medium heat until golden and crispy.
4. Make the Hollandaise sauce using two egg yolks (see page 29), reserving some water from the double boiler.
5. Blanch the spinach for 30 seconds in the water from the double boiler. Remove the spinach with a slotted spoon, then press out the excess water, and place on a kitchen towel to drain some more.
6. Put the Hollandaise sauce back over the hot water to keep warm while you poach the four eggs (see page 35).

FINAL TOUCHES

7. Now for the fun part: plating these bad boys up. Place two halves of the English muffin on a plate, face up. Top each half with spinach, then bacon, then a poached egg.
8. Finish off with generous dollops of Hollandaise sauce and a pinch of herbed paprika salt.

Game Night

Chili Sweetcorn Fritters with Cilantro & Lime Crème Fraîche SERVES 6–8

These sweetcorn fritters are a snap to make—and you can pack as much heat as you'd like them to have. Perfect for a night of beer guzzling with the boys. Just change the type of chili or adjust the spice level to your liking, and at your own risk.

The heat of chili peppers, which comes from a chemical compound called capsaicin, is measured on the Scoville scale. Unlike what most of us have been told, most of a pepper's heat does not live in its seeds. Turns out it's concentrated in the white pith found near the stem of the pepper, and it spreads out through the ribs, seeds, and little blisters in the skin. You should test the heat of any pepper before cooking with it, or you run the risk of ending up with a dish that only that one crazy friend of yours would eat. Testing by biting off the tip is not only dangerous, but ineffective, as the tip has very little heat compared to the stem.

To counteract the heat, the lime crème fraîche dip has a nice, zingy, cooling effect. This is a good example of balancing out a dish by using contrasting flavors and textures. The tug-o-war between the heat from the chili and the cooling effect of the dip keeps your taste buds on their toes and makes for more interesting, more enjoyable eating.

EXTRA GEAR

Thermometer (optional)

INGREDIENTS

Neutral oil (vegetable or canola), for frying

Fritters

1 medium heat chili, chopped (or 1 tsp dried chili flakes)
½ white onion, diced
1 cup sweetcorn
½ tsp salt, plus extra to season
1½ cup self-rising flour
1 Tbsp corn flour
1 tsp black pepper
½ cup milk
2 Tbsp butter
6 oz cheddar cheese
½ cup cilantro leaves, chopped
1 tsp mixed herbs
2 large eggs

Dip

Juice and zest of 1 lime
1 cup crème fraîche or plain crème cheese
½ tsp cracked black pepper, plus extra to season

PREP

1. Prepare your chilies (see sidebar for safety practices) by chopping finely, and add to the mixing bowl. Wash your hands, knife, and cutting board afterward. If using fresh corn, boil in water for about 4–5 minutes, then remove from water and carefully slice it off the cob.

METHOD

Fritters:

2. Add oil to the pot until it is about 4 inches deep. Start heating the oil, aiming for a temperature between 320°F / 160°C and 350°F / 180°C (see sidebar for notes). In a frying pan, fry the onion in the butter until soft. Add the corn, fry for a further 2 minutes, and then season with a pinch of salt.

3. To make fritters, combine the flour, corn flour, salt, and pepper, and mix. Add the milk, and whisk to form a batter. Add the contents of the pan to the batter and mix through.

4. Use a teaspoon to form little balls, and gently drop them in the oil. A few might burn or go soggy, but fear not—that is part of the process of getting better with practice.

5. Fry the balls in batches until golden brown, and remove from the oil with a slotted spoon. Season with a little extra salt immediately, and drain on paper towels.

Dip:

6. Reserving a little of the lemon zest for garnish, mix all the ingredients for the dip together, and place in a small bowl.

FINAL TOUCHES

7. Serve the fritters in a large flat plate or serving platter. Garnish the dip with lemon zest and a little extra black pepper, and serve.

NOTES:

CAUTION: While some chili peppers are relatively harmless, some will burn the daylights out of you. When working with chilies, always wash your hands thoroughly afterwards, and never touch your eyes or other . . . um . . . sensitive body parts until you have given your hands a good scrub. Even better, it is advisable to use rubber gloves when handling hot peppers.

The heat of the oil is crucial to successful deep frying. Too cold, and you'll end up with a pale, soggy mess; too hot, and the fritter's surface will burn before the inside is cooked. If you don't have a thermometer, drop little bits of flour mixture into the oil to see how it behaves. If it sinks to the bottom with very little bubbling, the oil is too cold. If it boils furiously and you see smoke, it is too hot (and you may be about to burn your house down).

Bear in mind that as you drop cold batter into the oil, the overall temperature will drop, so don't fry too many fritters at a time. Similarly, if you leave the oil on heat without any fritters in it for too long, it will overheat. Check regularly if you are unsure, and get into a rhythm that keeps the oil (and your stress) at optimal levels.

Bruschetta Tomato Salsa & Guacamole

SERVES 6–8

Bruschetta is a summertime favorite of mine—easy, cheap, and an excellent way to take advantage of fresh seasonal vegetables like tomatoes. It's one of my go-to snacks for barbeques or pool parties.

The bread can be partially toasted beforehand. The toppings will also get better on standing (whether you use tomato salsa and guacamole like I did or decide to come up with your own). That means you can do most of the prep work before your guests arrive and pop out a batch of these beauties at a moment's notice.

EXTRA GEAR

Food processor (optional)
Wire cooling rack (optional)

INGREDIENTS

Marinated tomato salsa

7 oz cherry tomatoes
½ clove garlic
¼ red onion
½ tsp brown sugar
3 Tbsp olive oil
1 Tbsp balsamic vinegar
3–4 basil leaves
¼ tsp salt
Cracked black pepper

Guacamole

1 avocado, mashed
2 Tbsp lime juice
¼ onion, chopped
¼ cup cilantro leaves
¼ cup red pepper, chopped
¼ chili pepper of medium heat
¼ cup olive oil
1 Tbsp paprika
1 Tbsp crème fraîche
1 tsp salt
Cracked black pepper

Bread

1 loaf sourdough bread
Olive oil, to drizzle
Garlic clove
Salt
Cracked black pepper

NOTES:
Don't toast the bread hours before your guests arrive—it will lose its crunchiness. Ideally, you want the bread to come fresh out of the oven and cool down for 10 minutes until just above room temperature before you start adding toppings.

PREP

1. Preheat the oven to 350°F / 180°C.

2. Wash the tomatoes, then slice into halves and then quarters. Peel and chop the garlic and onion.

METHOD

3. Add the ingredients for the marinated tomato salsa to a mixing bowl, and mix through.

4. Add the ingredients for the guacamole. Use a food processor to incorporate all the ingredients together, if you have one; otherwise, just go at it with a fork or a whisk.

5. Slice the bread. The slices should not be too thick, but sturdy enough to hold the toppings.

6. Place bread slices on a baking sheet and drizzle with olive oil. Place the tray in the oven and bake for 20–30 minutes until golden brown, turning the slices over every 10 minutes.

7. Once the bread is out of the oven, cut a garlic clove in half and rub the slices of bread with it, being careful not to burn yourself. Use a kitchen towel to hold the bread if you need to.

FINAL TOUCHES

8. Place the slices of bread on a serving platter and add your toppings.

9. Be generous, but don't overdo the toppings or most of it might end up in your guest's lap.

10. Finish off with a sprinkling of salt and black pepper on top.

Cheesy Twisters SERVES 6–8

Golden, buttery pastry entwined with that culinary match-made-in-heaven—tomatoes, olives, and cheese. This is beer-drinking sustenance at its best!

My favorite part is the cheesy bits that melt out onto the baking tray and turn dark and crispy. Cheese candy is a beautiful thing.

EXTRA GEAR

Food processor (optional)
Pastry brush
Pizza cutter (optional)
Wire cooling rack (optional)

INGREDIENTS

14 oz frozen puff pastry (the kind made with real butter, if you can)
7 oz sun-dried tomatoes
7 oz olives
1 tsp rosemary
1 clove garlic
1 egg
7 oz grated cheddar cheese
Flaky sea salt

NOTES:
Let these cool on a cooling rack, or stand them up vertically to form a tepee of sorts. This way, the moisture in the pastry can evaporate freely from all sides as it cools to keep the pastry nice and crispy.

PREP

1. The best way of thawing frozen puff pastry is to take it out of the freezer and leave it in the fridge overnight, the day before you plan on using it. In a rush, take it straight from freezer to a plate or cutting board, and leave it at room temperature. How long it will take to be ready will vary greatly depending on the temperature wherever you are, so you'll need to check it every 30 minutes or so. You want it to be firm yet bendable when you start rolling it out, not hard (still frozen) or too soft (when it is too warm, the butter will start melting).

2. Preheat the oven to 340°F / 170°C.

3. Puree the sun-dried tomatoes and olives separately in a food processor. If you don't own one, chop them up as finely as you can with a chef's knife.

4. Finely chop the rosemary and garlic together.

5. Pop the egg in a bowl, add a splash of water to thin the egg wash out a bit, then whisk it up with a fork.

METHOD

6. Roll out the pastry to about a tenth of an inch thick, and divide into three pieces. Brush with the egg wash.

7. Spread tomato puree on one piece, olives on another, and the garlic and rosemary mixture on the last. Sprinkle half of the grated cheese over the three sheets.

8. Fold each layer over itself, and cut into long strips about an inch wide using a pizza cutter or a sharp knife. Twist the strips a couple of times, lay them down on the silicon paper, and brush with egg wash again.

9. Top with the rest of the cheese, and bake until golden brown. It should take between 10 and 15 minutes.

10. Remove from the oven and pop the twisters on a cooling rack for a couple of minutes before serving.

FINAL TOUCHES

11. Sprinkle flaky sea salt over these guys while they cool. The variation in seasoning caused by the irregular crystal sizes keeps things interesting.

Bourbon Chicken Liver Pâté with Red Onion Marmalade SERVES 6–8

Liver. Love it or hate it . . . um, actually who am I kidding? Liver is delicious.

I am a firm believer that the majority of people who fall into the "I hate liver" camp were presented with a piece of badly cooked liver at some point in their lives, and that sealed the deal.

The soft, luxurious texture of liver is one of its main selling points, unless you forget to trim it properly or overcook the poor thing. Then it's just plain disastrous. I don't know too many people who enjoy picking pieces of membrane out from their teeth or eating a dried-out, grainy, gray mass.

Let's try and avoid all that, shall we, and do it the right way. Making liver pâté is one of the easiest ways to ensure a good texture and, thus, overall good experience of the dish.

EXTRA GEAR

Food processor

INGREDIENTS

Chicken liver pâté

7 oz chicken livers
Milk, to cover
½ yellow onion
1 clove garlic
2 Tbsp olive oil
Salt
Cracked black pepper
2 Tbsp Bourbon, plus extra to taste
1 tsp thyme
2 Tbsp red wine vinegar
2 Tbsp brown sugar
¼ cup cream
2 Tbsp butter, melted (plus extra to seal the pâté)

Onion marmalade

3 Tbsp olive oil
2 sprigs of thyme
1½ cup red onion, sliced
Pinch salt
2 Tbsp white wine vinegar
3 Tbsp brown sugar
40 cl or 2 shots bourbon
Pinch cinnamon

NOTES:

It's really important not to overcook the livers, and to trim them properly prior to cooking. Taking your time with these two activities will result in a much better end product.

PREP

1. Pop the livers out of the container into a small bowl, and cover with milk. Soak for 1 hour.

2. Next, we need to trim the livers. Remove from the milk, and pat them dry with paper towels before placing them on a cutting board. Using a sharp paring knife, cut off the hard, white, stringy bits of connective tissue. You can (gently) pull the membranes covering the livers off with your fingers. Take your time—chicken livers are very delicate, and you don't want to obliterate them with clumsy cuts.

3. Peel the onion and garlic. Slice the onion and mince the garlic.

METHOD

Chicken liver pâté:

4. Pop a nonstick pan over high heat, and add the olive oil.

5. Season the livers with salt and pepper. When the oil is hot, add the livers and fry until browned. It should take about 2 minutes. The livers should still be pink inside but browned on the outside. If you overcook them, the texture will become grainy. Add the bourbon to the pan, and simmer for 2 minutes.

6. Remove the livers from the pan. Add the chopped onion to the pan, and fry until slightly browned. Next, add the garlic and thyme. Fry for another minute, then deglaze the pan with the vinegar. Cook out the vinegar for a minute or so, then add the brown sugar and simmer for 2 minutes, stirring constantly.

7. Add the cooked onion mixture and chicken livers to a food processor, along with the cream and 2 Tbsp of melted butter. Blend until smooth, then have a taste, and adjust seasoning as needed. Add a splash more bourbon if you are feeling boozy.

8. Spoon the mixture into a serving dish, level the surface with the back of a spoon, and allow to set in the fridge for 30 minutes.

9. Melt the extra butter (you need enough to seal the top of the pâté), and allow to cool slightly.

10. Gently pour the melted butter over each pâté, just enough to completely cover it. Pop them in the fridge for at least 2 hours, preferably overnight, as they will develop better flavor.

Onion Marmalade:

11. Add the olive oil to a small saucepan on medium heat. Add the thyme, onions, and a pinch or two of salt, then fry until the onions are soft, adding a splash of water if it starts to stick to the bottom of the pan.

12. Add the vinegar and sugar, and cook for a minute while stirring. Next, add the bourbon and cinnamon, and cook on low heat until "jammy."

13. Remove from heat, allow to cool, and set in the fridge until ready to serve.

FINAL TOUCHES

14. Serve with melba toast (see page 246) or crackers.

Blackened Corn on the Cob with Chili & Cilantro SERVES 4

Look, I love sweet corn season just as much as the next guy, and few things can beat sinking your teeth into an ear of corn that is slathered with butter. Problem is, it can get boring pretty quickly, especially if you eat as much corn as I do.

This recipe is a great way to shake things up by adding some heat and flavor to the party. Lime and cilantro are old friends, bringing zesty freshness to the buttery corn. Use your favorite kind of chili, and adjust the quantities to suit your spice threshold.

Just make sure you have plenty of beer around to cool things down with. We all know it's essential to stay properly hydrated while engaging in strenuous activities like watching sports on television.

EXTRA GEAR

Wooden kebab sticks

INGREDIENTS

4 ears of sweet corn
1 large chili pepper of medium heat
1 scallion
¼ cup cilantro leaves, plus extra to garnish
1 tsp crushed coriander seeds
3 limes, zested and juiced (plus extra to garnish)
5 oz butter
1 Tbsp olive oil
Salt
Cracked black pepper

PREP

1. Bring a large pot of water to a boil.

2. Remove the husks and silk from the corn, and boil for 10 minutes. Then drain the corn, and cut in half.

3. Chop up the chili, scallion, and cilantro, and add to a bowl. Add the crushed coriander seeds and the juice and zest of two limes. Mix through, and divide into two batches.

METHOD

4. Heat a large frying pan on medium high heat, and add the butter and oil. Once the butter is foaming, add the corn halves, and fry for 3–4 minutes.

5. Add half of the herb mixture into the pan, and cook for a further 3–4 minutes, turning with the tongs to achieve even color as you go.

6. Add the other half of the herb mixture, mix well, then turn off the heat.

7. Remove, spike the corn with kebab sticks, and serve.

FINAL TOUCHES

8. Garnish with a few extra cilantro leaves, season with salt and pepper, and add the zest and juice of the last lime.

Panko-Crumbed Zucchini Sticks SERVES 6–8

Panko is a Japanese-style breadcrumb commonly used in Asian dishes, but it has become more and more popular in Western cooking. Its texture is more flaky than regular breadcrumbs, and it absorbs less oil, making it perfect for breading fried foods when you want to reach maximum crunch.

It works really well on these baked zucchini sticks—the soft, rich moisture inside the zucchini contrasting with a crunchy outer layer. Paired with zingy ginger dipping sauce, you have yourself a win.

INGREDIENTS

7 medium-sized zucchini (give or take)
2 cups panko crumbs
2 oz grated Parmesan cheese, plus more to garnish
2 eggs
Salt
Cracked black pepper

Dipping Sauce

2 tsp crushed ginger
2 Tbsp soy sauce
2 Tbsp honey
1 Tbsp sesame oil

NOTES:
You can also deep-fry the zucchini sticks after breading them if that's more your thang.

PREP

1. Preheat the oven to 400°F / 200°C.

2. Cut off the ends of the zucchini, and slice into batons about a ½ inch thick.

3. Mix the panko crumbs and Parmesan cheese together in one plate, and season with salt and pepper.

4. Whisk the eggs together in a bowl, and season with salt and pepper.

METHOD

5. Using one hand for wet ingredients and the other for dry ingredients, double-bread the zucchini. Dip each slice in the egg first, shake off the excess, then coat with the breadcrumbs. Repeat the process so you get a double layer of breading on each piece of zucchini.

6. Arrange the zucchini sticks on a baking sheet lined with parchment paper. Bake for about 20 minutes until golden brown, turning them over halfway through.

7. Mix all the ingredients for the dipping sauce together, and pour into a small dipping bowl.

FINAL TOUCHES

8. Grate a little more Parmesan over the top, and sprinkle with a touch more salt.

Me, Myself, and I

Mac & Cheese SERVES 6–8

Mac & cheese is a favorite the world over, but there is really no excuse for preparing the premade version of "mac & cheese in a box." Sure, some of those inventions are surprisingly delicious, but it's a sad day in our collective culinary consciousness if most people can't outcook a factory-produced box of preservatives.

I like to add a little extra crunch to this classic by topping it with breadcrumbs before baking. Experiment with different kinds and ratios of cheese to suit your palate, and ditch the ready-made for the really-good.

INGREDIENTS

Cheese sauce

2 cups grated cheddar
2 cups grated mozzarella
1 cup freshly grated Parmesan

Topping

1 cup breadcrumbs
1 cup mixed cheese (made from the three-cheese mix above)
2 tsp mixed Italian herbs
Handful of cherry tomatoes, sliced in half
Salt

Macaroni

2 Tbsp salt
1 lb macaroni

4 cups white sauce (page 21)

PREP

1. Preheat the oven to 400°F / 200°C.

2. Mix all three cheeses together in a big mixing bowl with your hands.

3. To make the topping, add one cup of the cheese mix to a separate mixing bowl along with the rest of the ingredients for the topping, and mix with your hands. Season with salt. Set aside.

4. Prepare the white sauce (page 21), and leave it in the pot it was prepared in.

METHOD

5. To make the macaroni, get a large pot of water boiling, and add kosher salt. Add macaroni to the boiling water and cook according to the instructions on the pack, but take away 2 minutes from boiling time. Stir for the first minute of cooking. Drain and set aside.

6. Add the leftover cheese mix to the white sauce and stir over low heat until smooth and combined. Add a little milk if the cheese is having trouble melting into the sauce or if the mixture becomes too thick. You want it to be smooth, creamy, and still pourable.

7. Return the macaroni to the pot. Pour over the cheese sauce, and mix well. Then, pour this mixture into a baking dish.

8. Add the topping mixture over the top, and bake for 30–50 minutes until the top is golden brown and crispy.

FINAL TOUCHES

9. Nothing much to do here—dig in!

Grilled Cheese Sandwiches with Tomato & Rosemary Soup

SERVES 4

When it comes to quick, cheap, easy, and delicious, few things can go head to head with a grilled cheese sandwich. With crispy, crunchy, buttery bread and a gooey cheese center, what's not to like? Pair that with a hot bowl of homemade tomato soup, and you'll have yourself one kick-ass meal.

Up until recently, I've been making these in a sandwich press, and then I learned the frying pan method. Sure, both methods produce grilled cheese sandwiches, but the frying pan method truly reigns supreme. Let me show you how it's done.

EXTRA GEAR

Stick blender

INGREDIENTS

Tomato and rosemary soup

2.2 lb / 1 kg ripe tomatoes
3 Tbsp balsamic vinegar
3 sprigs of rosemary
6 cloves of garlic in skin
2 Tbsp olive oil
2 cups water
Salt
Cracked black pepper

Finishing ingredients

1 Tbsp Sriracha
½ tsp smoked paprika
1 tsp white wine vinegar
1 tsp brown sugar
Salt
Cracked black pepper

Grilled cheese sandwiches

2 cups grated cheddar cheese (depends how cheesy you want to go)
½ cup salted butter (same story)
8 slices of sourdough bread

NOTES:
A nonstick frying pan is the easiest way to go here, but a well-seasoned cast iron pan produces the best results.

PREP

1. Preheat oven to 400°F / 200°C.

METHOD

2. To prepare the soup, slice the tomatoes and lay them out in a roasting dish with the rest of the ingredients for the tomato and rosemary soup. Roast for about 30 minutes.

3. Add the entire contents of the roasting dish, as well as all the finishing ingredients, to a high-speed blender, and blend until smooth. (If you like a really smooth soup, strain through a sieve.) Set aside.

4. To prepare the sandwiches, grate the cheese, and cut the butter into cubes (I like to cut them into one-tablespoon-sized cubes).

5. Heat the pan over medium-low heat. Place one tablespoon of butter into the pan. As soon as the butter has melted, place two slices of bread in the pan facedown, and swirl them around with the spatula.

6. Cook the bread until golden on the bottom (about 2 minutes), then flip them over. Add the other tablespoon of butter into the pan, and swirl the bread again.

7. Carefully place the grated cheese on one slice of bread, spreading it as evenly as you can. Flip the other slice of bread over and place on top of the cheesed-up bread, golden side down.

8. Cook the bread until crispy and golden on both sides, flipping every 30–60 seconds and very gently pressing down the sandwich with the spatula.

FINAL TOUCHES

9. Heat up the soup on the stove, and serve with your grilled cheese sandwiches.

Mushroom Risotto

SERVES 4

Risotto is one of the classic Italian staples that everyone should know how to cook. You can make any flavor of risotto your heart desires; the trick here is in the cooking technique.

I was lucky enough to learn the technique from Roberto Pietrella, a generous local Italian chef who took me under his wing. I've heard about plenty of "quick risotto" recipes, but I believe sometimes it's better to follow the traditional methods. If it ain't broke, don't fix it, and all of that.

So go on, put on some opera music, and employ your best fake Italian accent. It all adds to the character of the dish!

EXTRA GEAR

Medium-sized pot or high-walled frying pan (a wider base with walls at least 4 inches high)

INGREDIENTS

10 cups vegetable stock
1 oz dried porcini mushrooms
1 yellow onion
7 oz oyster mushrooms
7 oz portobellini mushrooms
2 Tbsp olive oil
5 oz butter, divided in two portions
1 lb (about 3 cups) risotto rice (arborio or carnaroli)
¾ cup white wine
5 oz Parmesan cheese
2 tsp thyme leaves
Juice of half a lemon

NOTES:

Making risotto is a labor of love. It's not hard to do, but it requires your constant attention. Get yourself a glass (or two) of wine, ignore your phone for a while, and enjoy the moment.

You can buy ready-made stock, make your own out of leftover vegetables, or use bouillon cubes and hot water.

Keep the stock fairly hot on the side; you don't want to cool down the risotto every time you add a ladle of stock.

Risotto should be cooked on medium-high heat, about 8 on a scale of 1 to 10. If the risotto is burning, you are either not stirring enough or you need to add more stock.

When frying the mushrooms, make sure to do so in small batches. If you overcrowd the pan, the mushrooms will release too much water, preventing them from browning.

PREP

1. Heat up the stock, and add the dried porcini mushrooms. Let that steep for 20 minutes, then fish out the mushrooms, chop them finely, and add them back into the stock.

2. Peel and dice the onion. Slice the fresh oyster and portobellini mushrooms.

3. Prepare and lay out all your ingredients. You don't want to scratch around for something while you are supposed to be stirring.

METHOD

4. Add the olive oil and half the butter to the pot, and place on medium-high heat. Once the butter has melted and started foaming, add the diced onion.

5. In this case, we don't want the onions to overpower the flavor of the mushrooms, so don't let the onions brown. To prevent browning from happening, add a splash of water to the pot if the onions start to caramelize. Cook for 3–4 minutes until they go soft.

6. Add the rice and start stirring. From this point on, you are not allowed to leave the stove and stop stirring for longer than 15 seconds, so focus, ya hear?! You want to stir vigorously and "bruise" the rice, so it releases more starch. Make sure you stir it in all directions and get all the corners—no cutting corners, okay? This stage of the game is called *tostatura*, which means toasting the rice. Cook for 2–3 minutes.

7. Add the white wine, and keep stirring. You should see the liquid turn milky—that's the starch releasing from the rice. Don't worry about the strong alcohol smell; it will cook off soon enough.

8. When the wine has become absorbed into the rice, start with the stock. Add a ladle or cup of stock one scoop at a time, and keep stirring. When the stock has been fully absorbed, repeat. Continue until you have used up all the stock.

9. While you are doing this, fry the fresh mushrooms over medium heat in a little olive oil in a frying pan. Do this in batches to make it easier to brown the mushrooms. Once browned, set aside and start the next batch.

10. After about 7–8 minutes, start testing the rice. Try to bite through a grain with your teeth. You want a slight bit of resistance in the middle of the grain, but it shouldn't be hard to bite through or dry in the middle. Bear in mind that the risotto will continue to cook with the residual heat in the pan, so you want to take it off the heat a little before it's actually ready. When the rice is ready, add the fried mushrooms to the pot (leave a few aside as a garnish), and take it off the heat.

11. The final step is called *mantecatura*, which basically means stirring everything together. Add the remaining butter, Parmesan cheese, and thyme to the pot (leave a bit aside as a garnish), and give it all a good stir. Have a taste, and adjust seasoning as needed.

12. Allow the risotto to rest for a minute or two, then serve.

FINAL TOUCHES

13. Dish up the risotto and garnish with the extra fried mushrooms and thyme leaves. Top it off with a good squeeze of lemon juice and a generous grating of Parmesan on top. Enjoy!

Buttermilk Pancake Stacks with Bacon & Maple Syrup SERVES 4–6

Pancakes (or, as we call them in South Africa, *flapjacks*) can be as simple or elaborate as you wish. For this recipe, I am going to show you one of the most basic versions, and I'll leave it up to you to develop your own favorite twists (if this is not it).

EXTRA GEAR

Whisk or electric hand mixer

INGREDIENTS

1 pack streaky bacon
2 cups buttermilk
3 Tbsp melted butter (plus more for frying and to serve)
2 eggs
2 cups all-purpose flour
2 tsp baking powder
½ tsp salt
1 tsp white sugar
Maple syrup, to taste

NOTES:

The consistency of the batter will have an impact on the kind of pancake you end up with. Depending on the type of flour and size of eggs you use, you might need to adjust the quantities somewhat to get them just right.

A drier batter will generally make the pancakes rise higher (which could make it tricky to cook them all the way through without burning the outside), while a wetter batter will make them flatten out a bit more.

If the first ones are burnt, turn the heat down a little and try again. Getting the heat and timing right will require some practice, and the first few pancakes usually flop. So don't get discouraged! Practice makes perfect, and you get to eat pancakes while practicing. Score!

PREP

1. Preheat the oven to 400°F / 200°C. Line a baking sheet with aluminum foil. Once the oven is hot, arrange the bacon on the sheet and bake for about 15–20 minutes, then drain on paper towels.

2. Alternatively, you could cook the bacon in the pan. As long as there is bacon, all is well in the world.

METHOD

3. Turn the oven down to 212°F / 100°C, and place a clean baking dish inside.

4. Mix the buttermilk, butter, and eggs in a mixing bowl, then add the flour, baking powder, salt, and sugar. Whisk it all together with a whisk or electric hand mixer.

5. Over medium-high heat, drop some butter in the frying pan, and when it has melted wipe out the excess with a paper towel. Drop about two tablespoons of batter per pancake in the pan, leaving enough space between them, as they will flatten out a bit.

6. When you start seeing bubbles appear on the top of the pancake, they are nearly ready to flip. Wait until you see a good amount of bubbles, then flip them over. Cook for another minute, and finally place them in the baking dish in the oven to keep warm. Repeat until all the batter has been used.

FINAL TOUCHES

7. To serve, build stacks of pancakes with bacon and small knobs of butter in between, then drizzle maple syrup over the top. Dig in and enjoy!

Fish Fingers SERVES 4

Okay, so we all grew up eating ready-made fish fingers out of a box in the freezer. To be honest, I am thirty-five, and I *still* eat those guys every now and then.

I like to make most things from scratch because nine times out of ten you end up with something way more delicious—and often a lot cheaper. All you have to do is put in some effort.

If you have kids, you can make these over the weekend. Let them do the dirty work of breading the fish, and freeze them so they are ready to go. Kids love making a mess, so you might as well get some benefits this way.

EXTRA GEAR

Sieve
Deep plates or containers for breading

INGREDIENTS

Fish Fingers

2 cups dried breadcrumbs
2 tsp dried chives
Salt
Cracked black pepper
1 cup flour
1 lb skinless white fish fillets (choose fillets that are firm)
3 large eggs
Canola oil
1 lemon

Sauce

1 Tbsp mayonnaise
2 Tbsp plain double thick yogurt
1 tsp dried chives
1 tsp lemon zest
Salt
Cracked black pepper

NOTES:

Avoid using boxed breadcrumbs if you can. Either buy them from your local bakery or make your own by drying out old bread in a low oven. Crush the bread by pulsing in a food processor, or place the bread in a plastic bag and crush with a rolling pin.

You can make these ahead of time up until you start frying. They also freeze really well. Freeze them on a plate or tray, then pop them in a freezer bag.

If using frozen fish fillets, allow them to defrost overnight in the fridge.

PREP

1. Sift the breadcrumbs in a sieve to divide them into two portions—one finer and one coarser. Place the crumbs on two separate plates.

2. Add a teaspoon of chives, and a good pinch of salt and pepper to each plate of crumbs. Mix through.

3. Pour the flour on another plate, and season with salt and pepper. Mix through.

METHOD

4. Slice the fish into finger-sized strips, dredge in the flour, and shake off any excess. Lay the fingers out on a plate, and place in the fridge to cool for 10–15 minutes.

5. Beat the eggs with a fork and a pinch of salt. Using one hand for wet ingredients and the other hand for dry ingredients, double-bread the fish. Dip the fish in the egg, allowing excess to drip off, then coat it in the finer portion of breadcrumbs. Repeat a coating of egg, and then coat in the coarser breadcrumbs.

6. Place the coated fish in the fridge again, and cool for 15 minutes.

7. Add a tablespoon of canola oil to the pan, and fry the fingers in batches on medium heat until golden brown all over. Remove from the pan and drain on paper towels.

FINAL TOUCHES

8. To make the sauce, mix all the ingredients for the sauce together, and serve in small bowls with the fish fingers (or just spoon some on each plate).

9. Cut the lemon into wedges, squeeze some juice over the fingers, and add a wedge to each plate.

Potato Rösti SERVES 4–6

The Swiss are mightily clever folks. First off, they gave us the Swiss Army Knife, that iconic tool without which MacGyver would have died a horrible yet spectacular death in the first episode, making the rest of the series fairly pointless.

These clever individuals from the land of cheese and chocolate were also responsible for bringing Velcro, Turbochargers, and LSD into the world. Male strippers, car enthusiasts, and Jimmy Hendrix fans have been thankful ever since.

Potato rösti is another clever Swiss invention. What to do if you really want pancakes, but all you have is a potato? Make a potato pancake, of course! Röstis are traditionally made with only potatoes, but you can easily add other vegetables into the mix to keep things interesting, like we will be doing here. You basically have a blank canvas, so throw whatever you feel like on there (but maybe hang back on the Cheetos).

INGREDIENTS

Rösti

3 medium size potatoes
1 medium zucchini
2 small scallions
1 baby leek
1 Tbsp fresh parsley, chopped
2 tsp of chives, chopped

Toppings

¼ cup fennel, finely shaved (with a knife or a mandolin)
1 Tbsp olive oil
1 Tbsp lemon juice
Pinch of chili flakes
Salt
Cracked black pepper
2 Tbsp neutral oil
2 inches of chorizo
¼ cup crème fraîche
A few sprigs of mint
Couple of chives, cut into 2-inch batons
Pinch of cayenne pepper or smoked paprika

PREP

1. Peel the potatoes, and top and tail the zucchini. Grate both of them into a bowl. Slice the scallions and baby leeks nice and fine, and add them to the bowl. Add the chopped parsley and chives.

2. Add the shaved fennel (you can shave fennel with a mandolin or a knife) to a bowl with the olive oil, lemon juice, and chili flakes. Set aside to marinate.

METHOD

3. Mix the potato mixture well, season with a strong pinch of salt and pepper, then mix again. Heat a pan on medium heat, then add about a teaspoon of neutral oil.

4. To make the first rösti, take half of the mixture and squeeze out most of the liquid. Add it to the pan, and pat it into a round cake about half an inch thick.

5. Fry until golden on the bottom, about 2 minutes. Place a plate on top of the pan, and while holding them together, carefully (and without hesitation) flip them over so the rösti lands on the plate. Slide the rösti back into the pan and cook on the other side for a further 2 minutes. Repeat.

6. Slice the chorizo into slices, then halves. Fry in a little olive oil until crispy.

FINAL TOUCHES

7. To serve, top the rösti with the chorizo, marinated fennel, dollops of crème fraîche, mint leaves, chive batons, and a pinch of cayenne pepper or smoked paprika.

Weeknight Winners

Spaghetti Aglio, Olio e Peperoncino SERVES 4

Spaghetti aglio, olio e peperoncini, translated as *spaghetti with garlic, oil, and chilies* is one of the easiest dishes you will ever make. Anybody can cook it to an acceptable standard, but to master it takes a measure of skill and practice. It is also quick to make, as the sauce takes roughly the same amount of time as the pasta needs to cook. It is also cheap; you probably have all the ingredients in your kitchen cupboard already.

Don't be fooled, though. Recipes that use a few basic ingredients require that you treat each individual ingredient with respect and cook it to perfection in order for the dish to shine. Do that well, and you will have a beautiful dish at the end. Do it while distracted, and you will probably burn the garlic and overcook the pasta. Be the first guy; don't be the second guy. Nobody likes him.

The only thing that takes a bit of time is making the breadcrumbs. I make batches of these whenever I have stale bread around, so I always have homemade breadcrumbs (see page 247) at hand. I suggest you do the same.

EXTRA GEAR

Large pasta pot
Large frying pan, capable of holding a pound of cooked pasta
A coffee mug
Colander

INGREDIENTS

Salt, for boiling water (plus extra to season)
6 cloves of garlic
3 small mild chillies, or whatever heat level you desire
¾ cup of good olive oil
1 lb dried spaghetti
Cracked black pepper
1 cup homemade breadcrumbs (see page 247)
½ cup of grated Parmesan, plus more to garnish

NOTES:

Be generous with the salt in the water used to cook the pasta. It is essential to season the water well, as the pasta will absorb this water. Adding more salt to the cooked pasta afterward does not have the same effect.

I usually just eyeball it, but around 2 tablespoons of table salt for every 3 quarts of water should do the trick.

METHOD

1. Get a large pot of salted water going on high heat. Read the instructions on the back of the pasta packet. Take note of the suggested cooking time, and subtract 2 minutes.

2. Peel the garlic. Slice the garlic and chili finely. Add the garlic, chili, and oil to an unheated frying pan, and set aside.

3. Add the pasta to the pot of water, and gently stir it around until all the pasta is covered with water.

4. Now put the pan with the oil on medium heat. We want to infuse the oil with the garlic and chili. If you see browning happening, reduce the heat, and add 2 tablespoons of the pasta water to the pan.

5. Scoop some of the pasta water into a coffee mug, and set aside. When the pasta has finished cooking for our modified cooking time, drain it in a colander. Do not rinse it! Add the pasta to the frying pan, along with half the mug of pasta water. Season the contents of the pan with a little more salt and pepper.

6. Toss around in the pan with tongs, and cook for 2 minutes. Add the breadcrumbs and Parmesan, and toss through for 30 seconds.

FINAL TOUCHES

7. I like to serve pasta dishes family-style, i.e., a big serving bowl in the middle of the table that everyone helps themselves to.

8. If you want to get fancy and plate the food yourself, use a large carving fork to twirl the pasta around, place the fork horizontally on the plate, then gently pull out the fork and let the pasta sit. You'll get a neat roll of spaghetti (after some practice). Garnish with more Parmesan and black pepper on top.

Beer-Battered Fish & Chips SERVES 4–6

Fish and chips is an early example of "fusion cuisine," where culinary traditions of two or more cultures are combined to create something new and more than the sum of its parts. Fried fish was reportedly introduced in England by Jewish immigrants from Spain and Portugal. It was served as is, or with a baked potato. The origins of chips (French fries) are still hotly disputed between the French and the Belgians.

Be that as it may, the first fish and chips shops combining these two traditions was opened in London in the 1860s, and it was an instant smash hit among the British working class. It has grown from strength to strength since those humble beginnings and is now a British institution loved the world over.

EXTRA GEAR

Chip cutter (optional)
Deep fryer or large pot
Slotted spoon or spider strainer

INGREDIENTS

2 Tbsp salt (for water)
8–10 large potatoes
Oil for deep frying
1 lemon
4–6 fillets fresh fish (of your choice)
Salt
Cracked black pepper
Flour for dusting

Batter

1½ cup self-rising flour
1½ cup beer
1 tsp salt

PREP

The day before:

1. Prepping the chips the day before makes for much less work when your guests arrive. Get a pot of water boiling and add the salt. Cut the potatoes into chips using a chip cutter. If you don't have a chip cutter, cut them by hand using a chef's knife. First, cut the round parts off the potato on all sides so you end up with a rectangle. Cut the potato into strips that are a ½ inch wide, turn over to lay on the rectangular side, and then cut again into ½-inch-wide chips.

2. Boil the chips for 7 minutes, then remove from the boiling water and lay out on a tray to cool. Once the chips have reached room temperature, pop the tray in the freezer.

3. Repeat the process until you run out of potatoes.

The day of:

4. Heat oil in the deep fryer to 350°F / 180°C.

5. Slice the lemon into wedges.

METHOD

Batter:

6. Mix all ingredients for the batter until just combined; there should still be small lumps of flour about.

Fish:

7. Season the fish well with salt and pepper and coat in flour, shaking off the excess.

8. Working with one hand only, hold the tail end of the fish (if there is one), and place in the batter. Carefully pull it out again, letting all the excess batter drip off.

9. Immediately pop into the hot fryer at 350°F / 180°C.

10. Cook until golden on both sides.

FINAL TOUCHES

11. Season with a little more salt and pepper, then serve with lemon wedges.

Cannelloni SERVES 4–6

Cannelloni is an Italian classic, much like lasagna, its slightly more popular cousin.

Lasagna is a little easier to make, as you don't have the hassle of filling the pasta tubes, but both are equally delicious. The traditional recipes for each are probably accompanied by a long list of what exactly should be used as fillings for each kind of pasta (you know how Italians can get about their food), but in truth I use them interchangeably and fill them with whatever I feel like at the time. For this recipe, I use a basic tomato-based meat ragù. Other popular fillings are spinach and ricotta, mushrooms, seafood, etc.

As with lasagna, cannelloni can be prepared up to the point right before baking and then frozen, which makes it great for weeknights when you don't feel like cooking. Just remove the cannelloni from the freezer, thaw, and pop into the oven to bake. No mess, no fuss.

EXTRA GEAR

Piping bag (optional)
Reusable herb infuser (or cheesecloth and kitchen twine)

INGREDIENTS

Meat ragù

1 yellow onion
2 medium carrots
1 stick celery
8 oz portobellini mushrooms
2 cloves garlic
2 Tbsp olive oil
½ lb ground beef
½ lb ground pork
6 oz tomato paste
½ cup dry white wine
1 14-oz can chopped tomatoes
2 cups beef stock
1 tsp Worcestershire sauce

***Flavor bomb* (bouquet garni)**

2 whole star anise
2 cloves
2 bay leaves
2 sprigs of rosemary
2 sprigs of thyme

Tomato Sauce

2 14-oz cans chopped tomatoes
2 tsp mixed Italian herbs
2 Tbsp Sriracha
1 tsp salt
4 cups white sauce (page 21)
1 cup Parmesan, grated
Parsley, to garnish

NOTES:

Cannelloni is an excellent way to use up any leftover foods you have lying around. Just make a filling of your choice (spinach and ricotta also works really well), smother it with tomato and white sauce, top with cheese, and bake.

If you have freezer space, make double the amount of tomato sauce and meat ragù, and label and freeze the extras. These ingredients can be used in a truckload of other dishes, so prepare ahead and save yourself some time and effort.

To use frozen cannelloni, take them out of the freezer and put in the fridge a day or two before for optimal defrosting. If you are in a hurry, you can speed things up by defrosting them in the microwave or on low heat in the oven.

To make a *bouquet garni* (or flavor bomb, as I like to call it), either use a reusable herb infuser or wrap and tie the appropriate ingredients in cheesecloth. The idea is to impart flavor from these ingredients during cooking, while being able to easily remove them once done. No one wants to bite into a whole clove thinking it's a chunk of meat. I've done it; it's not fun.

PREP

1. Chop the onion, carrots, celery, mushrooms, and garlic for the meat ragù finely. Keep in mind that you have to stuff these ingredients into the small cannelloni tubes. Add the flavor bomb ingredients into a herb infuser ball, or wrap and tie them up in cheesecloth.

METHOD

Meat ragù:

2. The ragù takes the longest to cook, so let's start with that. Add a little olive oil to a pot and fry the chopped onions, carrots, and celery for 10–15 minutes until softened and just starting to brown on the edges. Tip the contents of the pot into the mixing bowl.

3. Put the pot back on the heat with a splash more oil if the pot looks dry. Add the mushrooms, garlic, and a generous pinch of salt, and cook for 10 minutes until the mushrooms have released their water and start to brown. Tip the contents of the pot out into the mixing bowl again.

4. Fry the beef and pork in batches, adding the cooked batches to the mixing bowl as you go. Cook the meat until a dark brown color forms on the surface (no, dude, gray is not brown, and black is not brown, either), breaking up the chunks of meat with the wooden spoon as you go.

5. When all the meat is cooked, add the tomato paste to the pan, and fry it for 2–3 minutes, stirring with the wooden spoon to prevent it from burning. Deglaze the pot with wine, and add the contents of the mixing bowl back into the pot.

6. Add the tomatoes, beef stock, Worcestershire sauce, and the flavor bomb. Simmer on low heat for 1½–2 hours. Check in on it every now and then, and add a bit of water if things get too dry.

7. Remove the flavor bomb. Remove from heat and allow to cool.

Tomato Sauce:

8. Add the tomatoes, herbs, Sriracha, and salt to a saucepan, and simmer for 10–15 minutes.

Cannelloni:

9. Preheat the oven to 350°F / 180°C.

10. Add the tomato sauce to the bottom of a baking dish. Fill the cannelloni tubes with the meat ragù and arrange in the baking dish, in two layers if need be.

11. Top with white sauce, and grate the Parmesan on top. Bake for 25–30 minutes until a knife easily pierces the cannelloni tubes.

12. If the top hasn't browned enough by the time the tubes are cooked, pop the dish under the broiler for a few minutes to get some color on that Parmesan. Remember: color equals flavor!

FINAL TOUCHES

13. Garnish with a few leaves of fresh parsley.

Bulgur Wheat Surprise SERVES 4

I like me some long, slow cooking recipes—the more complex the better. Those recipes that require you to start working stuff three days in advance? Sign me up. Slow smoke a large chunk of meat for ten hours while drinking beer? I'm your man.

Well, this is not one of those recipes. In fact, I'm not even sure it's an actual recipe, as such.

It's basically just a name that rolls off the tongue a bit better than "Whatever You Have in the Fridge at the Time with Bulgur Wheat." This is what I cook when I'm lazy, when I've spent my weekly takeout allowance already—and it's only Wednesday.

Bulgur wheat is pretty rad. I love the nutty flavor and the fact that it's so easy to cook (just soak it in boiling water while you fry up the rest of the stuff). Use whatever vegetables you have on hand, and surprise yourself. I never cook it exactly the same way twice.

INGREDIENTS

Salt, for boiling water
1 cup medium ground bulgur wheat
3 medium carrots
1 onion
3 medium zucchini
8 oz button / portobello mushrooms
½ yellow bell pepper
½ red bell pepper
Olive oil
1 lb ground beef
2 large handfuls of baby spinach
A pinch of nutmeg
A squeeze of lemon juice
Cracked black pepper

PREP

1. Boil 2 cups of water. Add the boiling water, a pinch of salt, and the bulgur wheat to a bowl. Stir through, and set aside.

2. Grate the carrots. Slice the onion, zucchini, mushrooms, and bell peppers.

METHOD

3. To get the best flavor out of the ingredients, I like to fry them in batches, transferring each one to a large mixing bowl as I go. If you add too many ingredients (or too much of one) to the pan at once, they will release too much water, and you'll soon be braising, not frying (see instructions on how to brown meat properly on page 23).

4. Add olive oil to a large pan over medium-high heat. Fry the sliced vegetables, starting with the onions, carrots, and peppers first, seasoning as needed. Mushrooms and zucchini contain a helluva lot of water, so add these next and fry in smaller batches.

5. Fry the meat until properly browned, and add to the mixing bowl. Deglaze the pan (see instructions on page 25) with a splash of water, then add all the ingredients back to the pan. Bring it all up to heat and stir through.

6. By now, the bulgur wheat that was set aside should have soaked up the water. Add that to the pan, as well, discarding any excess water if you can. Add the baby spinach leaves on top, with a pinch of nutmeg. Don't worry if it looks like a mountain of spinach in the pan—in a minute or so, the spinach will wilt and blend in with the ingredients, taking up very little space. Push the leaves down into the rest of the ingredients to speed things up. Fry all of that for 2–3 minutes more, stirring as you go.

FINAL TOUCHES

7. Have a taste and adjust seasoning as needed with a pinch of salt and pepper. Squeeze a bit of lemon juice over, mix through, and serve.

Orange, Garlic & Cilantro Chicken

SERVES 4–6

This easy-to-cook dish is great for those nights when you really don't feel like spending too much time and money in the kitchen.

Cilantro is kind of a weird one—some people love it, while others hate it. Try this out for yourself and see into which camp you fall.

EXTRA GEAR

Casserole dish, just wide enough for the chicken to fit in a single layer

INGREDIENTS

- 1 yellow onion
- 5 cloves garlic
- 2 Tbsp honey
- 1 tsp paprika
- 2 tsp ground coriander
- 1 tsp cumin
- 1 cup orange juice
- 2 Tbsp olive oil
- 2 lb chicken drumsticks and thighs
- 2 oz butter
- Salt
- Cracked black pepper
- ½ cup cilantro, chopped (plus a little more for garnish)

NOTES:
If you don't want to use the oven, make this dish on the stove top. Use a pan that is large enough to hold all the chicken pieces and liquid. Cook on medium heat, turning every 5 minutes. You may need to add more liquid if things get too dry before the chicken is cooked.

PREP

1. Preheat the oven to 350°F / 180°C.
2. Peel the onion and the garlic. Slice the onion, and roughly chop the garlic.
3. Mix the honey, paprika, coriander, cumin, and orange juice in the mixing jug.

METHOD

4. Place the frying pan on medium-high heat, and add the olive oil and butter. Season the chicken pieces with salt, and fry them in the pan in batches, taking care not to overcrowd the pan. We are not trying to get them cooked through here, just nice and brown on the outside. Remove the browned pieces of chicken from the pan and set aside. Repeat until all of the chicken pieces have been browned.
5. Add the onions and garlic to the pan, and cook for 2–3 minutes until they start to brown. Add the orange juice mixture, bring to a boil, and turn the heat down to a simmer. Cook for 5 minutes to reduce the liquid a bit.
6. Add the chicken to a casserole dish, and pour the sauce over. Bake in the oven for 30 minutes, turning the pieces halfway through with tongs.

FINAL TOUCHES

7. Add the chopped cilantro leaves on top of the chicken, and turn to coat again with sauce and leaves.
8. Serve with rice, mashed or baked potatoes, or whatever else you fancy.

Pork Schnitzel with Cheese & Beer Sauce

Pork schnitzels are cheap and easy to make at home, perfect for quick weeknight dinners. The contrast between the smooth, creamy, cheesy beer sauce complements the crunchy pork, making for grade-A eating.

If you don't feel like bashing the meat to flatten it out yourself, ask your butcher to lend a hand—that's what they're there for.

INGREDIENTS

Schnitzel

4 deboned pork chops, fat trimmed off (about 6 oz each)
1 cup flour
2 cups breadcrumbs
Salt
Cracked black pepper
1 Tbsp dried (or fresh, chopped) sage
3 eggs
2 Tbsp neutral oil

Beer Sauce

1 yellow onion
2 cloves garlic
2 Tbsp olive oil
2 Tbsp salted butter
2 Tbsp flour
1 cup beer
1 cup cream
1 cup grated strong cheese
Sage leaves, to garnish (optional)
Salt
Cracked black pepper

PREP

1. Place the chops between 2 layers of wax paper or plastic wrap, and pound it with the flat side of a meat mallet, rolling pin, or the bottom of a frying pan to quarter-inch thickness. Peel and slice the onions and garlic.

METHOD

Schnitzel:

2. For breading, set up a production line. Prepare three separate bowls. In the first, add the flour. In the second, add the eggs, and whisk. In the third, add the breadcrumbs, sage, and a generous pinch of salt and pepper, and mix well.

3. Using one hand for dry ingredients and the other for wet ingredients, dredge the pork in flour, then egg, then breadcrumbs.

4. Add oil to the frying pan on medium-high heat, and fry the schnitzels until golden brown and crispy, about 3–4 minutes.

Beer Sauce:

5. Add the olive oil to a small saucepan on medium heat. Fry the chopped onion and garlic until browned. Remove from the pan and set aside.

6. Melt the butter in the pan, and add the flour. Whisk to form a smooth paste. Add the beer slowly while whisking vigorously until smooth. Next, add the cream, bring it up to a simmer, and add the cheese and whisk until smooth. Next, add the onion and garlic back in, along with salt and pepper to taste.

FINAL TOUCHES

7. If you want to be fancy with the garnishing, fry a few fresh sage leaves in the remaining oil in the pan. It will take a few seconds to pop and crisp up.

Meat
Matters

NOTES:

You want top quality fresh beef from a reputable butcher, not the frozen stuff from the supermarket. Tell your butcher you are planning on making steak tartare. If he is worth his salt, he will respect you much more and give you the best meat for the job.

Gaining your butcher's respect can result in you getting better meat in the future, which is never a bad thing.

Steak Tartare SERVES 2–4

Steak tartare is one of my all-time favorite dishes. To me, the mark of a good cook is to be able to pull off this dish. There is no place to hide bad ingredients or technique with heavy sauces or condiments; its beauty is in its simplicity. Start with the best ingredients you can find, don't cut corners when preparing it, and you will reap the rewards.

The star of the show here is the beef, and the extra ingredients I list below are really just guidelines. Make this recipe your own by adjusting quantities and adding or removing ingredients that suit your palate. That's part of the beauty of this dish: there are so many variations, and every cook who serves it puts his own spin on it.

The idea of eating raw meat may be unsettling to some people, but come on—grow a pair and give it a go. Think of it as "steak sushi."

INGREDIENTS

10 oz of the best beef you can find, trimmed of any sinew
2 Tbsp onion, diced
2 Tbsp flat leaf parsley, chopped
2 tsp pickled cucumber, diced
2 tsp brined capers, drained and chopped
2 large egg yolks
Dash Worcestershire sauce
Dash tabasco sauce
2 tsp Dijon mustard
12 thin slices of French baguette, toasted
Salt
Cracked black pepper

PREP

1. It is essential to keep the meat cold all the way through the process, so I suggest taking two stainless steel bowls, filling one halfway with ice or ice water and placing the other on top. You can place the meat in the top bowl to ensure it stays cold as you work.

METHOD

2. Chop the meat up by hand. The size of the dice is up to you—some prefer it very fine while others like it chunkier. Try out different-sized dices until you find your favorite, then stick with that. The most important thing is to keep the meat cold while you work.

3. I usually serve steak tartare in one of two ways. I either make a sauce by whisking together all the ingredients (except for the meat), gently mixing the sauce in with the meat before plating; or I serve everything prepped individually in small bowls, which allows my guests to mix and eat the tartare in whichever way they want.

4. A cool presentation trick is to leave the egg yolk in half an egg shell, propped on top of the meat in a little indentation. Many people choose not to eat raw egg, and this gives them the option of adding it themselves.

5. Season the tartare with salt and pepper right at the end, as the salt will start breaking down the meat.

FINAL TOUCHES

6. Plating is very important with a dish like this—raw meat can easily look unappetizing if not presented well. Get your inner artist on and plate a masterpiece!

PAPRIKA
CELERY SEEDS

Grilled Rib Eye with Steak Salt SERVES 2

Any self-respecting man should be able to cook a decent steak, period. Even if you are vegan (let's not get into that here), when push comes to shove, you should be able to cook steak for an esteemed guest, potential boss, foxy romantic interest, or a gaggle of foreign dignitaries (depending on your aspirations).

When it comes to grilling steak, a hotly disputed topic is whether you should flip steaks often or only once during cooking. I tried the flip-once method for a while but wasn't happy with the results. The steaks had a great crust, but the outer layer was dried out by the time the inside was suitably cooked. So, I've always been in the flip-often camp, without really understanding why, until I came across a brilliant article on SeriousEats.com by J. Kenji López-Alt. With meticulous detail, he experimented with both methods and shared the result with his readers in his inimitable "food-geek science made accessible to normal folk" manner.

Turns out I was right all along! Flipping often (30 seconds to a minute) over medium-high heat allows for more even cooking, and as an added bonus steaks cook up to 30 percent faster this way! The idea is that there is less of a drop in temperature between the side currently facing the heat and the one facing away. That way, you increase the internal and external temperature of the steak gradually, resulting in more evenly cooked, juicier meat.

Once the steak nears your preferred internal temperature, crank the heat up and sear both sides for that rich, dark-brown crust we all adore. López-Alt calls this method the *reverse sear*, and I've been using it ever since. I used to sear first, then finish off on cooler heat, but the reverse sear is a safer and more effective way to go about it.

In terms of flavoring, the next must-have skill to master is making your own spice mixes. You don't deserve bragging rights for your steaks if you smother them with store-bought seasonings and sauces; they'd probably taste the same as your neighbor's down the road. Salt and pepper is certainly enough when you have a beautiful grass-fed, dry-aged piece of meat to work with, but when you want to boost the flavor of a steak, a custom blend of steak salt is the ticket. Making your own spice mixes is simple to do, and it allows you to customize flavors to your liking. Once you have the guys begging you for your recipe, full bragging rights are automatically assigned and should be suitably utilized.

NOTES:

Cheap electric coffee grinders make excellent spice grinders. Buy one dedicated to spice grinding, or you'll end up with weird flavors in your coffee. To clean it out, grind up uncooked rice.

Buy your steak from a butcher shop if you can. Grocery stores don't carry the best meat. Their primary concern is making as much profit as possible. Among other things, they tend to not age steaks long enough, as it reduces its shelf life. Developing a relationship with a butcher with a passion for meat is the best way to go here.

I highly suggest you get your hands on a copy of J. Kenji López-Alt's James Beard-award-winning cookbook *The Food Lab: Better Home Cooking Through Science*, or check out his articles on The Food Lab on SeriousEats.com. The man is without a doubt my go-to online resource whenever I am doubtful of the best way to cook a certain ingredient. I am a bit of a fan (understatement of the book).

EXTRA GEAR

Mortar and pestle (or electric coffee grinder)
A grill capable of maintaining two heat zones
Thermapen or similar instant read probe thermometer

INGREDIENTS

2 pieces 1½- to 2-inch-thick de-boned rib eye steaks
Olive oil

Steak salt

2 tsp coriander seeds
1 tsp celery seeds
2 tsp black pepper
2 Tbsp kosher salt
1 tsp brown sugar
1 tsp instant coffee
1 tsp paprika
1 tsp dried parsley

NOTES ON DONENESS:
There are numerous ways to gauge whether steaks are at the right level of doneness. Personally, I poke them with my finger and "guesstimate" from there. In truth, the best way to do it is with an instant read probe thermometer, like the Thermapen by Thermoworks. Insert the thermometer in the center of the steak, and take a reading. Bear in mind that the residual heat in the meat will continue to cook it even when it's taken off the grill, so you want to remove the steak when it's a couple of degrees below your intended target.

Here is an internal temperature guide:

- Rare: 120°F / 49°C
- Medium rare: 130°F / 55°C
- Medium: 140°F / 60°C
- Medium well: 150°F / 65°C
- Well Done: 160°F / 71°C

PREP

1. Make the steak salt. Using a mortar and pestle or spice grinder (see sidebar), grind up the coriander seeds, celery seeds, and black pepper. Mix this in with the rest of the ingredients for the steak salt.

2. Set your grill up—with a zone on high heat and another on medium heat.

METHOD

3. Rub the steaks with olive oil on all sides, then season generously with the steak salt you just made. Start them off on medium heat, flipping every 30 to 60 seconds. Make sure to give the edges a couple of turns on the heat, as well. You want to render out and cook the fat; nobody likes eating uncooked animal fat.

4. When the steaks are about halfway to your desired temperature (see sidebar), it's time to get some color on those bad boys. Move them over to the high heat zone and watch them like a hawk, turning every 30 seconds. We want to get a rich dark-brown color and a crispy surface. A little bit of charring (blackening) is okay, but too much will make the steak go bitter.

5. Get the steak off the grill when it hits the target—a few degrees under your desired internal temperature. The residual heat left in the exterior after searing will be enough to lift the internal temperature the last couple of degrees.

FINAL TOUCHES

6. Because the reverse sear method does not leave the surface of the meat in contact with intense heat, it's not really necessary to rest the steaks. In a way, you're already resting it every time you flip it over.

7. Serve these bad boys with your favorite side dish—think French fries, baked potatoes, or roasted vegetables.

Guinness & Tomato Beef Short Rib SERVES 6

Beef short rib is one of my favorite cuts of meat for low and slow cooking. While this cut is way cheaper than steak or tenderloin, if you learn to cook it correctly, you will end up with a meal so good you may never buy a tenderloin again!

The key is in the cooking technique. I used to cook my short ribs low and slow in a Dutch oven, but after recently acquiring a slow cooker, I've found slow cooking to be a much more hassle-free and foolproof method. And since most of the readers this book is aimed at could certainly do with as much foolproofing as possible, I decided to list the slow cooker version here.

EXTRA GEAR

6-quart slow cooker / crock pot
Large sieve / colander / chinois
potato masher

INGREDIENTS

Beef short rib

2 medium onions
2 celery stalks
3 medium carrots
3 lb beef short rib
Salt
Canola oil (or another vegetable oil)
1 Tbsp dried Italian herb mix
2 star anise
Cracked black pepper
1 6-oz tin tomato paste
2 Tbsp honey
1 Tbsp red wine vinegar
1 22-oz bottle of Guinness, or any other dark stout (leave extra for deglazing)
2 Tbsp corn flour
Water

Mashed Potatoes

3 lb potatoes
Salt
3 Tbsp butter
½ cup of cream (or milk)
Cracked black pepper

Gremolata

1 large handful flat leaf parsley
3 cloves garlic, chopped
1 lemon, zested
2–3 Tbsp olive oil

PREP

1. Peel the onions, and cut into half-inch slices.
2. Wash the celery, trim off stray leaves, and cut into half-inch slices.
3. Peel the carrots (if you wish; I prefer leaving the skin on), and cut into 1-inch chunks.

NOTES:

Slow cookers tend to create a lot of liquid during cooking. This means you don't need to cover the food completely with liquid when you start, as more liquid will accumulate during the cooking process.

Introducing more liquid will also mean your seasoning will be diluted, and the food could taste bland. To fix this, we strain and reduce the cooking liquid afterward to make a sauce, taking into account that the seasoning will become more prominent as the sauce reduces.

For this reason, wait until the sauce is at the consistency you want before doing a final seasoning check, as you can't remove salt once added but can always add more later.

Once the short rib is cooked, it will be extremely succulent and tender, which unfortunately also means it will fall apart very easily. Handle it with care if you are trying to keep them whole. I suggest using tongs as well as a spoon held underneath to support and lift them out of the sauce.

METHOD

Beef short rib:

4. Season the meat generously with salt. Place a frying pan on medium-high heat and add a splash of oil. Fry the meat in batches on all sides until browned. Place the cooked meat in the bottom of the slow cooker or crock pot.

5. Once all the meat has been browned, add the chopped onions, celery, and carrots to the pan, and fry for about 6 minutes. When you see some color developing, transfer to the slow cooker.

6. Deglaze the pan with a dash of Guinness, and transfer all that liquid to the slow cooker (for deglazing instructions, see page 25).

7. Add Italian herbs and star anise to the slow cooker. Season the contents of the slow cooker with 2 teaspoons each of salt and black pepper.

8. In a mixing jug, dissolve the tomato paste, honey, and vinegar in the beer, then add it all to the slow cooker.

9. Set the slow cooker on low heat, and cook for eight hours. When done, carefully remove the meat from the pot and strain the sauce through a sieve. Place the meat back in the slow cooker.

10. Add the sauce to a saucepan. Reduce by half over medium-high heat, then turn down the heat to a slow simmer. In a separate bowl, mix the corn flour with roughly 3 tablespoons of water, and stir well until smooth. Add to the sauce, and stir through.

11. Let the sauce simmer for 5–10 minutes. Taste and adjust the balance and seasoning as needed. Set the slow cooker on low so it can keep the meat warm while you prepare the mashed potatoes.

Mashed potatoes:

12. Peel and halve the potatoes. Add to a pot, cover with water, and add a generous pinch of salt. Bring to a boil, and cook for 20 minutes. Test the potatoes by prodding one with a fork. If the fork goes in and out of the potato without much resistance, they are ready.

13. Drain the potatoes in a colander and transfer to a mixing bowl. Add the butter and the cream. Mash the potatoes with a masher.

Gremolata:

14. Gremolata is a magical thing. It works *perfectly* with rich, meaty dishes like this, and it is incredibly simple to make. Chop the parsley and garlic (how fine is up to you), and pop in a small bowl along with the lemon zest and olive oil. Mix through.

FINAL TOUCHES

15. To plate the dish, start with a generous helping of mashed potato, and carefully place the short rib on top. Pour over some of the delicious sauce we made earlier.

16. Finish off with a few small blobs of gremolata scattered across the dish.

17. Have a seat, and enjoy the fruits of your labor.

Beef Carpaccio SERVES 4

Beef carpaccio is a classic Italian dish and a staple in my "slightly fancy summertime appetizer" repertoire.

I used to think it best left to professional chefs in high-tech kitchens. It is crucial that the slices of meat be paper thin, and my first few attempts were nowhere near that. I went online (Google is your friend) and found that one should put the meat in the freezer briefly (to firm up the meat, not freeze) just before slicing, but still my knife skills weren't up to the task. Some more reading and experimenting later, I came up with this technique that is easy as pie. Actually, pies are *way* trickier.

If you have issues in your head about eating raw beef, man up and give it a go. I dare ya.

EXTRA GEAR

Rolling pin
Good bread knife

INGREDIENTS

7 oz beef tenderloin
1 baguette (a day or two old is better)
Extra virgin olive oil (the good stuff)
Salt
Freshly cracked black pepper
1 lemon
2 oz Parmesan cheese (not the pre-grated, packaged stuff; the real deal)

PREP

1. Wrap the tenderloin in plastic wrap and place it in the freezer. Check on it every 20 minutes or so. The meat will firm up, but we don't want it to actually freeze. The moment you feel ice crystals forming, take it out immediately.

2. Remove the plastic wrap. Slice the meat into slices as thinly as you can safely manage. Don't worry about getting them too thin at this stage; we will flatten them out later. Just make nice, even cuts.

3. Roll a sheet of plastic wrap out on a work surface, but don't cut it off the roll. Leave the roll out in front of you. Lay the slices of meat on the plastic, and make sure to leave enough space between them as they will expand quite a bit. Don't put them too close to the side of the plastic, either. Roll the cling film back over the meat, and squeeze out any air pockets. Cut off the plastic roll, and set aside. With a rolling pin, gently roll out the meat, and lightly tap down any stubborn bits. You want the meat to be thin but not smashed to pieces.

4. Repeat with the rest of the meat. Finally, roll up these sheets of plastic, and place in the fridge until ready to serve.

METHOD

5. Preheat the oven to 350°F / 180°C.

6. Place the serving plates and platter into the fridge if you have space to cool them

NOTES:

Tell your butcher you are making carpaccio. He'll give you the best cut for the job—and his opinion of you will climb a few notches.

You want the best-quality beef you can get your hands on; it makes all the difference. The cool thing is that you need very little meat, so you can afford to splurge on the high-end stuff.

Don't "saw" at the meat by going back and forth with the knife. You want two smooth movements. First, start with the tip of the knife just leaning over the edge of the meat farthest from you, pushing down gently but firmly while you move the blade forward and down. That should get you at least halfway through. Then, keeping the tip of the blade on the board, pull back and apply pressure downward as you go.

The meat can be flattened between two sheets of plastic wrap ahead of time, then rolled up and stored in the fridge a few hours until serving.

7. Slice the baguette into slices as thin as you can, and lay them out on a baking tray. Bake for about 20 minutes, turning them over after 10 minutes. Keep an eye on these babies—you want a light-golden color with no burnt spots. Remove the slices from the pan, and allow to cool slightly. Now you're ready to assemble this masterpiece.

FINAL TOUCHES

8. Drizzle a little bit of olive oil over the serving platter, and season with a little bit of salt and black pepper. Unwrap the meat, and arrange next to the bread in a single layer on the platter.

9. Season the top of the meat with a little more salt and pepper. Slice the lemon into wedges, and squeeze just a drop or two on each piece of meat.

10. Drizzle with a little more olive oil, and finally make it rain with grated Parmesan using a fine grater. Dig in!

Porcini-Rubbed Prime Rib Roast SERVES 10–12

When it comes to roast beef, nothing beats the flavor, texture, and pure spectacle of a dry-aged prime rib roast on a festive table.

Dry-aged beef is very expensive, but it's totally worth it in my opinion. The flavor of the meat intensifies, and the fat takes on a nutty, creamy, almost buttery texture. Personally, I'd rather eat less meat than eat lots of mediocre meat. Luckily, we have access to top quality meats at affordable prices in my native South Africa.

Porcini (cep, penny bun, king bolete) mushrooms are culinary superstars, adored by food lovers the world over. During fall, my friends and I can be found hunting for them in forests at the foot of Table Mountain. We dry out the surplus for use throughout the year. The dried mushrooms can be reconstituted in water for use in soups and risottos, blitzed in a food processor to make porcini salt, or ground to a powder.

Foraging for mushrooms is risky business. That said, if you put in the effort and time required to learn how to identify mushrooms safely, and, more important, the deadly ones that look similar to the ones you are hunting, it is a highly rewarding activity. You can safely gather a variety of great-tasting mushrooms for free.

Because you will be spending a significant amount of money on a large chunk of top-quality dry-aged beef, I completely understand that cooking it may feel intimidating. What if you mess it up and waste all that money (and become the laughing stock of the family)? I don't believe we should let fear dictate the chances we take or do not take in life; that is no way of living.

The recipe below provides a foolproof method of cooking a perfect prime rib roast. When you pull this one off, you will be heralded as *The Meat Whisperer*, and songs will be sung about The Day of The Roast. Just be aware that this will mean you will be in charge of the roast at every large get-together from here on out (that is a cross I bear with honor).

NOTES:

While dry aging *can* be done at home, unless this is your passion and you are prepared to put in the time, money, and effort to learn how to do it correctly, it is best left to the professionals.

A "leave-in" thermometer is a handy tool to check the progress of the roast as it cooks. I have one with a base station outside the oven (to which the probe connects via cable) and a wireless receiver / monitor that I can carry around with me. That way, I can check on the roast from anywhere in the house without having to open the oven.

The only issue with leave-in thermometers is that they can be slightly inaccurate. Because the probe is metal, it conducts heat, so the exposed part of the probe will pick up the heat in the oven and transfer it to the inside of the roast. The meat surrounding the probe will therefore cook a little quicker and thus show a higher temperature than the rest of the meat. Just treat this as an early warning system, and use an instant read thermometer to check for 100 percent accuracy.

EXTRA GEAR

Roasting rack ("V" rack)
Kitchen twine
Roasting pan
Leave-in meat thermometer (optional)
Instant read meat thermometer (not negotiable; you need this)
Immersion blender or stand blender (optional)
Strainer / sieve

INGREDIENTS

Roast

1 "4-rib" dry-aged prime rib roast, about 9 lb (ask your butcher to "French trim" the roast and give you the trimmings to take home)
2 medium onions
3 medium carrots
2 ribs celery
Sprigs of whatever herbs you have around (thyme, rosemary, oregano, etc.)
2 Tbsp olive oil
Salt
Cracked black pepper
1 cup red wine (and more for a sauce, optional)
Flour or cornstarch, to thicken (optional)
Beef stock (optional)

Porcini rub

½ oz (about 5 Tbsp) porcini powder
2 Tbsp salt
2 Tbsp brown sugar
1 Tbsp cracked black pepper
1 Tbsp coriander seeds, crushed
1 tsp sweet paprika
1 tsp dried chili flakes

NOTES ON DONENESS:
See page 116.

PREP

1. Make some space in your fridge. Use up all your vegetables in preparation for the meat fest that is upon you, or drink the two shelves of beer you keep for emergency purposes. Place a wire cooling rack in the fridge, and put your roast on top of it (make sure it can fit). You may need to remove a shelf or two.

2. Mix all the ingredients for the porcini rub together, and rub it into the meat. Make sure you get it into all the nooks and crannies. Wrap the exposed French trimmed bones with aluminum foil.

3. Place the roast on the cooling rack, and leave overnight in the fridge. At first, the salt will pull out some surface moisture of the meat, but after an hour or two, the meat will start pulling that moisture back in, taking some salt with it, allowing the seasoning to get into the core of the meat instead of just lying on the surface layer. Spending the night in the fridge will also dry out the surface moisture, which will result in the formation of a crispier and more flavorful crust.

4. The next day, preheat the oven to 250°F / 120°C. Peel and slice the onions, carrots, and celery into chunks. Tie your herbs together with a kitchen string to form a basting brush.

METHOD

5. Heat a large pan to medium heat and add the oil. Pop the cut vegetables in the pan, and fry for 2–3 minutes. Transfer the vegetables to the roasting pan.

6. Season the meat trimmings with salt and pepper, and fry in the pan until brown. Deglaze the pan (see page 25) with a splash of wine, then add the rest of the wine along with the vegetables back to the pan. Bring up to a boil, then reduce the heat and simmer for 3–4 minutes.

7. Transfer the mixture to the roasting pan. Remove the roasting rack with the roast from the fridge, and place it in the roasting pan. Make sure the feet of the rack is stable on the bottom of the pan and not lying on top of any vegetables. The roast on the rack should be placed fat cap side up. Insert your leave-in thermometer (if you have one) in the center of the roast from the side.

8. Pop the roast in the oven, and have a beer—you've earned it. Cooking times will depend on a number of variables; that's why it's essential to use a thermometer. If you do not have a leave-in thermometer, you'll need to check it periodically with an instant read thermometer. Whenever you check it (every hour or so), dip your herb brush in the juices in the bottom of the pan, and brush the roast all over.

9. Bear in mind that the residual heat in the meat will continue to cook the roast even after you remove it from the oven, so you want to remove the roast from the oven about 5°F / 3°C below your intended target.

10. When the roast has reached the target temperature, remove the pan from the oven, lightly cover the roast with aluminum foil, and set aside to rest. Remove the vegetables and juices from the roasting pan, and set aside—you will be making a sauce of your choice (see below). Wipe the roasting pan clean, and put the roast back on the rack and inside the pan. Turn up the oven to 450°F / 230°C.

11. Once the oven is up to temperature, remove the foil, and use the herb brush to spread more of the pan juices that you set aside earlier on the roast. Place the roast back in the oven, and let it crisp up for about 10–15 minutes, watching it like a hawk. You want a nice, brown, crispy crust, but don't burn it, okay?

12. Now, you have a few options on what to do next with the contents of the roasting pan. The first option is to serve it as is, allowing your guests to pick out any vegetables or meaty bits they desire.

13. The second option is to blend it all together with an immersion blender or normal stand blender to make a sauce. Be sure to hold the top with a kitchen towel if using a stand blender, or you may end up with an interesting new paint job in the kitchen. If you want, you can thicken it up by whisking in a bit of flour or cornstarch and simmering it for about 5 minutes to allow the flour to "cook out."

14. If you want to be fancy, the third option is to make beef au jus (with juice). Strain the meat trimmings and vegetables, catching the juices and fat in a measuring jug. Allow to cool a bit. The juices will divide into two layers, beef juice at the bottom with a layer of fat on top. Scoop off most of the fat with a spoon or small ladle, but leave a little in there (now is not the time for dieting). Add the juices to a pan with a bit of beef stock and red wine. (The exact amounts are impossible to give you, as the amount of juices you collect will vary. Just wing it.) Bring that to a boil, then reduce the heat to a slow simmer. Let it simmer for about 5–10 minutes for the mixture to reduce—au jus is not thick like gravy; it's more like a slightly reduced broth. Finally, pour into a gravy boat or similar container.

FINAL TOUCHES

15. With as much fanfare and aplomb as you can muster, take the roast to the table, and get your good knife out. Debone the roast by running the blade down the inside of the bones, slightly angled toward the bone so it doesn't carve into the meat. Leave the bones and a knife somewhere on the table, and watch the "true" carnivores have at it. I for one love few things more than attacking a meaty bone with a pen knife in hand. Some of the tastiest pieces of meat are locked in between those bones, and I'll be damned if I'm going to let a little bit of effort or table etiquette get between us.

16. Once the roast is deboned, you basically have a slab or roasted rib eye in your hands. Carve off slices using smooth, even strokes; don't hack at it with short, jagged motions.

17. Another great idea is to serve the roast with a compound butter (to learn how to make one, such as anchovy butter, see page 27), which will go great with any piece of beef.

The Bacon & Cheese Burger SERVES 5

Here is where we separate the men from the boys. There are plenty of big mouths out there, all claiming to make the best burger around, so when the time comes to show your burger-making skills, you better have a good understanding of what makes a good burger. I really suggest you invest in a hand crank or electric mincer so you can buy decent cuts of meat in the quantities required and grind them to your liking.

There is no right or wrong way to make a burger. Different strokes for different folks. Some prefer the pure taste of beef with just salt and pepper; others prefer to add spices to enhance the flavor. Some add eggs and things like breadcrumbs as filler to keep the meat together. You probably grew up with one kind of burger and fervently believe that it's the best way to make a burger, but I urge you to explore other methods and learn something that may improve your own recipe—or at the very least show you where and how your recipe blows the others out of the water. Here are the most important things you need to keep your eye on:

CUTS AND TYPES OF MEAT

The first thing you need to decide is what kind of meat to use. A pure beef burger is a beautiful thing, but adding some pork certainly adds to the flavor. I like to go with a mixture of 70 percent beef, 30 percent other meat from time to time. In terms of cuts, I usually go for chuck or rib meat, or topside if I can't find either of those.

If you are unsure, ask your butcher what he recommends for burger making.

FAT-TO-MEAT RATIO

Getting the ratio of lean meat to fat is crucial in getting the flavor and texture right. In meat, fat is where the flavor and juice is, so make sure you add enough to your recipe. I generally tell the butcher to prepare a ratio of 70 percent lean meat to 30 percent fat. Your butcher should have extra fat in his shop—he trims it off while processing carcasses and primal cuts and typically uses it to make sausages or burgers. If you try the 70-30 mix and you find it too fatty, adjust the ratio to your liking. These are *your* burgers, after all.

METHOD OF COOKING

Most dudes would think that the best way of cooking a burger is on the grill, and it certainly is a mighty fine way of cooking (taking into account that larger amounts of beer need to be consumed to counter the heat).

The problem I have with cooking burgers on the grill is that a lot of the fat drips down into the flames, gone forever. Sure, you get some smoky flavor, but I don't think that's a good enough reason to let all that flavorful fat fall through the grates.

I believe that the most flavorful crust you can get on a burger is by cooking it in a pan. Letting the outside of the burger caramelize in its own fat just adds that extra kick of beefy flavor. Add a knob of butter to the pan just before you are done cooking, and baste the top of the burger by tilting the pan and spooning the juices over the top of the burger.

Using pans can be a bit impractical if you need to cook loads of burgers for a group. If you plan on doing this often, I suggest investing in a flat-top grill—they cook burgers like a dream.

BUN

As much as I generally like more robust bread, when it comes to burgers I feel the bun should play more of a supporting role and not try to take center stage too much. That said, the bun should be capable of carrying the burger patty you are building. If it's too soft and crumbly, the whole thing will fall apart. I like to toast the buns prior to assembling the burger. It adds a bit of crunch and prevents the bun from getting soggy too quickly.

CONDIMENTS

Pickles, mustard, onion marmalade . . . the list is endless. The main thing you are looking for here is a bit of crunch and tang, a touch of acidity to cut through the fattiness of the burger and the richness of the cheese.

CHEESE

When choosing a cheese for your burger, there are two things to consider—flavor and melting ability. As much as I love stronger cheese like mature cheddars, they don't melt very well, which means you won't get that gooey, cheesy goodness that, in my mind, is essential to a good cheeseburger.

Ask your cheese monger for advice on cheeses you can use, and mix and match them to get your signature mix. If you don't have the luxury of a good cheese monger in your area, sometimes the best thing to do is to use processed cheese slices. They melt really well, and, much as I hate to admit it, they taste pretty damn good!

EXTRA GEAR

Meat grinder (hand crank or electric)
Spice grinder or mortar and pestle
Kitchen scale
Burger press (optional, see textbox)
10 cellophane burger discs (2 per patty)
Electric beater

INGREDIENTS

Seasoning

1 tsp yellow mustard seeds
1 tsp black mustard seeds (or 2 tsp of either)
1 tsp coriander seeds
½ tsp celery seeds
1½ tsp salt
1 tsp garlic powder
1 tsp black peppercorns
1 tsp sweet paprika
1 tsp dried parsley

Burger Assembly

2.2 lb / 1 kg beef (70% lean / 30% fat)
12 rashers of streaky bacon
2 large tomatoes
3 medium pickles
10 slices of cheese
5 hamburger buns
1 head of crispy lettuce

Quick-Pickled Red Onion

2 medium red onion
½ cup white wine vinegar
1 tsp sugar
1 tsp salt

Secret Sauce

1 cup heavy cream
2 Tbsp bottled horseradish
2 tsp sweet paprika
½ tsp salt
½ tsp cracked black pepper

NOTES:

Track down a butchery supply store and get a steel burger press (that can take 7 ounces of meat) that most small-scale butchers use. While the plastic ones work, they tend to break after a while. The steel ones are built like a tank and should last you a lifetime. While you are there, get thin round cellophane discs that fit the size of the press. Placing one of these cellophane discs on either side of the meat before pressing the patties will help the patties release from the press and prevent them from sticking to one another.

If you don't have a burger press, you can form the patties with your hands.

NOTES:

You can freeze extra patties, but don't leave them out at room or fridge temperature for too long. Because we mix salt into the burger, the salt will break down the meat and change its texture. Freezing them as soon as possible delays this process a bit.

Everyone's tolerance for salt varies, so a burger that one man finds perfectly seasoned will be way too salty for another. Use my ratios as a starting point, and adjust the recipe to your liking.

The most crucial part of my burger-grinding and patty-making method is to keep the meat and fat as cold as you can throughout the grinding process until the patties are pressed. Ideally, you want it at a temperature *just* before it starts to freeze. I keep the extra cubes of meat that will be ground in the freezer for the most part. Check on the meat regularly. If you feel ice crystals forming, take it out of the freezer for a while, but it's crucial that you keep it as cold as possible. I freeze the metal head of my meat grinder overnight before making burgers, since the grinding process causes friction, which will heat things up.

The main reason I keep everything very cold (apart from food safety) is texture. If the fat gets warm, it will go soft and smear around the strands of meat as it comes out of the grinder, and we shall have none of that. You want the fat to come out of the grinder in firm white strands, clearly separate from the meat. This is essential to getting the texture of the burger just right. When you cook the burger, the fat will melt and distribute through the meat. This leaves little air pockets behind where the firm strand of fat was. First, this will give the burger a crumblier texture and help avoid hockey-puck syndrome (when the burger reduces in size through cooking to the size of a hockey puck). Secondly, some of the fat will stay behind in these pockets. As you slam the burger into your mouth, you will open the air pockets up and be rewarded with a blast of flavor juice (that may likely run down your chin), straight to the taste buds. You're welcome.

PREP

Burger Patties:

1. Place the head of your grinder in the freezer to cool. If you're using an all-metal hand crank grinder, just freeze the whole thing.

2. To start the seasoning, add the mustard, coriander, and celery seeds along with the black peppercorns to a dry pan with a heavy base. Heat the pan up and toast the seeds, continuously swirling them around in the pan. After about 2–3 minutes, you will smell their flavor intensifying. When they start to brown and pop, immediately remove from the heat and place on a plate to cool down. Once cool, grind them up in a spice grinder or mortar and pestle. Then, mix together with the rest of the seasoning ingredients.

3. Get the meat very cold (see sidebar), then slice into cubes small enough to fit into the hopper of your meat grinder. Sprinkle the seasoning you've just made over the meat, mixing through with your hands. Return the meat to the freezer to stay cold. This will help delay the process of the salt breaking down the meat fibers and ruining the texture.

4. Remove the grinder head from the freezer and attach to the base. Place a large mixing bowl under the outlet of the grinder. Get the meat out of the freezer and grind the cubes, turning the mixing bowl as you go to make space for the new arrivals.

5. Pop the meat back in the freezer while you get ready for pressing. Lay out five cellophane separator discs on a work surface, and keep five more on the side. Get the meat out, and use the kitchen scale to divide it into 7-ounce balls. Don't overwork the meat, just gently form into balls and place each ball between two cellophane discs.

6. Carefully place the press over each ball and press down, gently but firmly, to form a burger patty. Don't squash it. If you don't have a burger press, form the patties with your hands, pressing them down with a flat plate, then straightening up the sides with your fingers. If you don't plan on cooking these bad boys right away, it's best to freeze them ASAP.

Quick-pickled Red Onion:

7. Peel and slice the onions into either full- or half-circle slices. Mix the vinegar, sugar, and salt together in a mixing bowl, then add the onions. Stir with a fork every now and then to coat the onions with the pickling liquid.

Bacon:

8. Preheat the oven to 400°F / 200°C. Lay the bacon on a cookie sheet, and roast in the oven for 15–20 minutes until crispy. Turn the heat down to 350°F / 180°C.

Toppings:

9. Slice the tomatoes and pickles.

METHOD

10. Slice open the burger buns, and lay on a cookie sheet, cut side up. Toast in the oven at 350°F / 180°C for about 5 minutes until they start to brown and turn crispy. You could also panfry them in some burger fat for extra beefy flavor. Doing them all at once in the oven just makes things a little easier.

11. Fry the burger patties in a nonstick frying pan on medium-heat, about 2–3 minutes a side. As the fat renders out into the pan, baste the burger with its juices by tilting the pan and spooning the fat over the burger. Flip the patty one more time, top with a slice of cheese, and remove from heat after another minute. Repeat with the next patty. (You should have five slices of cheese left over.)

12. As you do this, prepare the secret sauce. Whip the cream in a large mixing bowl using the electric beater until stiff peaks start to form. Don't overdo it. Add the rest of the ingredients for the secret sauce. Beat for a few seconds more until combined.

FINAL TOUCHES

13. All right, let's build this sucker!

14. On the bottom half of the bun, spread a small amount of secret sauce, then cover with a layer of crispy lettuce. This will help keep the juices from making the bun soggy. Pop a patty on top, and cover with more sauce.

15. Add the rest of the toppings—tomatoes, pickles, and bacon—in whatever order you like, and pop another slice of cheese on top. Spread some sauce on the cut side of the top bun, and close that bad boy up.

16. Forget about table etiquette, manners, and all that. Grab the burger with both hands, and go at it. Make sure you have plenty of napkins around, as things tend to get messy, just like a good burger should.

Sunday Staples

NOTES:

I use tenderstem broccoli for this recipe, as I prefer its quicker cooking time and appearance. The recipe works for normal broccoli, too—just increase the blanching time by a minute or two, depending on the size of the florets.

Adding baking soda to the blanching water will help the broccoli retain its bright green color. Use roughly a teaspoon of baking soda for every gallon of water in the pot.

When blanching, it's essential to use enough water for the amount of vegetables you want to cook. Roughly one gallon of water for every pound of vegetables should do the trick. If you use too little water, the vegetables will cool the water down too much for effective blanching. You want the water to return to boil within one minute of adding the vegetables.

If you want to blanch the vegetables ahead of time and do the frying part later, drop the vegetables into a large bowl of ice water directly after cooking. This is called "shocking," and it will stop the cooking process. If you don't shock the vegetables directly after blanching, the residual heat will continue cooking the vegetables, which will result in an overcooked, mushy end product.

Sesame Broccoli SERVES 4

Kids grow up hating broccoli—it seems to be a fact of life. I was certainly no exception. As we grow older, though, we change—and so does our taste in food. I make a point of trying anything I used to hate as a kid from time to time and am often pleasantly surprised when I find myself actually loving this thing I used to hate.

There is, of course, another thing to consider: not all kids grow up with parents who cook well. I often see overcooked broccoli served at dinner tables. Boiled into submission for way too long, the poor vegetable has given up, leaching most of its flavor into the water and slumping down into a sad-looking mushy green mess. You can't blame a kid for hating the stuff.

This recipe will hopefully change your mind about broccoli. Let's give the poor guy a chance at redemption, shall we?

INGREDIENTS

½ lb tenderstem broccoli
1 Tbsp white sesame seeds
1 tsp baking soda
1 Tbsp sesame oil
1 Tbsp olive oil
Juice of ½ lemon
Salt (use a nice finishing salt like Maldon if you can)

PREP

1. Get a pot of boiling water going.

2. Trim the broccoli, removing any woody bits normally found at the bottom of the stem.

METHOD

3. Place the frying pan on medium heat, and add the sesame seeds. Toss the contents of the pan frequently to prevent the seeds from burning. Once the seeds are browned, remove the pan from the heat, and tip the seeds out on a plate to cool.

4. Add baking soda to the boiling water, and then pop in the broccoli. Add the sesame oil and olive oil to the pan, and place it back on medium heat.

5. After 1½ minutes, remove the broccoli from the water with the tongs, shake off excess water, and put them in the pan. Fry for 1–2 minutes in the oil until you get some color on there. The broccoli should be tender but still have a little bit of crunch to it. If it turns out too soft for your liking, reduce blanching time the next time you cook this.

FINAL TOUCHES

6. Squeeze lemon juice over the cooked broccoli, then sprinkle with the sesame seeds and some salt.

Slow-Roasted Pork Shoulder with Apples SERVES 10–12

Crispy crackling with juicy slices of pork. Soft, sweet, caramelized vegetables on the side. The smell of roasted deliciousness wafting through the house. Yeah, you know what I'm talking about—it's time for Sunday lunch.

People are often intimidated by the prospect of cooking large hunks of meat. We all have that one aunt who can't cook to save her life but who insists on wowing the world with her culinary abilities at every possible opportunity. In reality it's not hard at all once you get the hang of it. Meat cooked on high heat over an extended period of time makes the muscle fibers tense up, which squeezes out the moisture. Bad, bad idea.

Instead, you want to cook a roast low and slow first, which allows it to cook through gently without losing too much moisture. Then you crank up the heat to crisp the skin right at the end. Simple enough, right?

EXTRA GEAR

Mortar and pestle or electric spice grinder
Roasting pan

NOTES:
Ask your butcher to score the skin of the pork shoulder for you—they are pros at this sort of thing.

INGREDIENTS

Pork Shoulder

1 whole, bone-in, skin-on pork shoulder (roughly 8–10 lb)
1 yellow onion
4 carrots
1 leek
2–3 green apples
1 small fennel bulb
2 tsp dried Italian herb mix
4 bay leaves
¼ cup olive oil (plus extra for rubbing)

Seasoning

2 tsp fennel seeds
2 tsp cracked black pepper, plus extra to season
2 Tbsp salt, plus extra to season
1 tsp celery seeds
1 tsp brown sugar
1 tsp paprika
1 tsp dried (or fresh, chopped) sage

PREP

1. Preheat the oven to 320°F / 160°C.

2. If the skin of the pork shoulder was not scored by the butcher, do it yourself with a sharp paring knife, just barely cutting through. You don't want to cut all the way through the fat and into the meat.

3. Chop the onion, carrots, and leek into chunks. Peel the apples, and cut into quarters. Slice the fennel.

4. Grind the fennel seeds, and mix with the rest of the seasoning ingredients.

METHOD

5. Add the chopped onions, carrots, leeks, apples, and fennel, along with the herbs and olive oil, to a roasting dish. Mix well, and season with salt and pepper.

6. Drizzle some olive oil on the pork, and rub with your hands to completely coat the pork. Add the seasoning and rub that into all the nooks and crannies, too.

7. Place the pork, skin side up, on the vegetables in the roasting dish, and cover with aluminum foil, tucking it in around the edges of the pan.

8. Cook for 3 hours at 320°F / 160°C. Remove the tinfoil, and baste the meat with the sauce using a spoon. If you can, move the pan to the bottom rack of the oven.

9. Increase the heat to 350°F / 180°C, and cook uncovered for a further for 45 minutes to an hour, until the meat has browned and the pan juices have reduced.

FINAL TOUCHES

10. Serve with smashed roast potatoes (page 177) and sides of your choice.

Chicken, Corn & Mushroom Pie SERVES 6–8

Aaah, chicken pie, king of comfort foods (depending on who you ask, of course; people can be very particular about their comfort).

The great thing about this recipe is that the chicken and corn is cooked in the same broth, which is then used to make the sauce that binds the pie ingredients together. This way, all of the flavor that has been cooked out of the chicken and corn is retained in the final pie, with lip-smacking results.

EXTRA GEAR

Strainer (optional)
Pastry brush

INGREDIENTS

1 sheet puff pastry
1 roasting chicken, whole or equivalent pieces
8 cups (½ gallon) chicken stock
2 cobs worth sweetcorn (or 200 g of baby corn)
2 Tbsp olive oil
6 oz bacon
8 oz portabellini mushrooms
1 yellow onion, peeled and sliced
½ cup white wine
1 egg

Sauce

7 Tbsp (3½ oz) butter
⅘ cup (3½ oz) flour
1 cup cream
Salt
Cracked black pepper

NOTES:
A pie bird / pie vent allows the steam to escape from the filling when baking, resulting in crispier pastry. If you don't have one, just make a few slits in the pastry with a knife.

PREP

1. If you are using frozen puff pastry, allow to defrost in the fridge overnight or at room temperature for about 2 hours if you are in a hurry.
2. If using a whole chicken, cut it up into pieces that will fit into the pot. No need for precision here; it will all be picked apart anyway.
3. Add the chicken pieces to the pot and lightly brown for 10 minutes. Next, add the stock and bring to a boil. Reduce the heat to a simmer, and cook until chicken is soft, roughly an hour.
4. Remove chicken pieces from the pot, and allow to cool. Cook the corn in the stock until soft, then remove. Strain the stock if necessary, and reduce over low heat until you have 3 cups worth of stock—this will be reserved for use to make the sauce later. Scoop off any foam that forms on top of the stock while cooking.
5. Pick apart the chicken pieces, making sure to get rid of all the bones. Put the chicken in a mixing bowl.
6. Preheat oven to 350°F / 180°C.

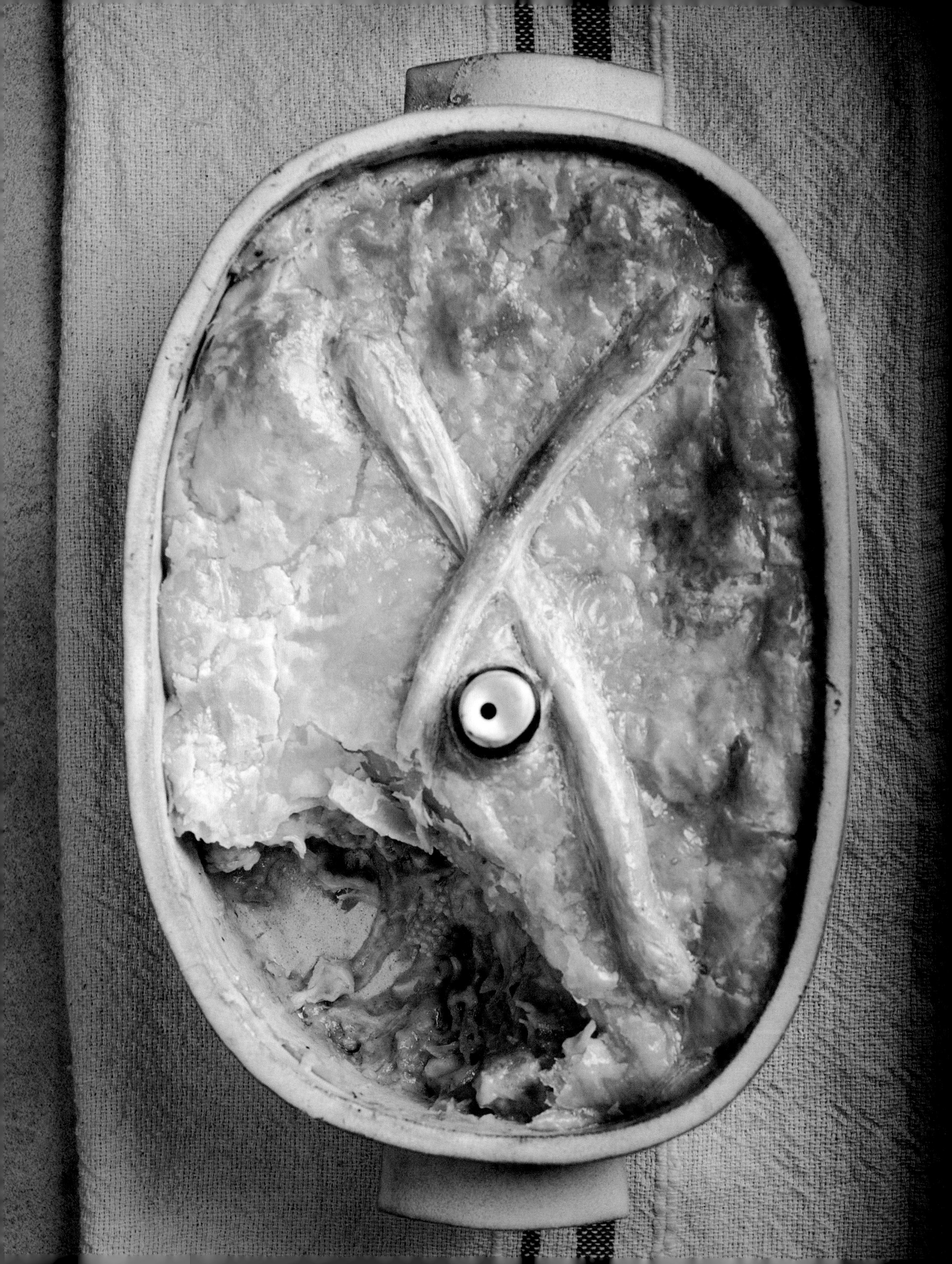

METHOD

7. Place a frying pan on medium heat and add the olive oil. Fry the bacon until crispy, and add it to the mixing bowl.

8. Fry the mushrooms in batches (taking care not to overcrowd the pan; you don't want too much juice to leak), and add to the mixing bowl.

9. Fry the onions until browned, and deglaze the pan with white wine. Simmer for 3 minutes, and add to the mixing bowl. Remove the corn from the cob, and add to the mixing bowl.

Sauce:

10. Melt the butter in a small saucepan, and add the flour. Whisk this into a paste, and cook for 2–3 minutes. Remove from heat, then slowly pour in the 2 cups of chicken-and-corn stock while whisking vigorously. Add the cream, and whisk until smooth. Season with salt and pepper to taste, and cook for another 5 minutes while stirring.

11. Add the sauce to the other ingredients, and mix well. Taste and adjust seasoning as needed, then spoon the mixture into your baking dish.

12. Roll out the puff pastry on a floured surface with a rolling pin until wide enough to cover the baking dish. Lay over the baking dish, and gently push down the sides with your fingers and trim off the excess.

13. Beat the egg. Brush the top of the pastry with the egg, and bake for 30 minutes until golden brown.

FINAL TOUCHES

14. Serve with a side salad or more boiled corn on the cob.

Hasselback Potatoes

SERVES 6–8

Hasselback potatoes are said to have originated from the Restaurant Hasselbacken in Stockholm, Sweden. They were very popular in the eighties, and for good reason—they are bloody delicious. I think it's high time they make a comeback.

By slicing open the potatoes, you expose more surface area of the potato to the fat and heat, crisping more of it up for better flavor and texture. They're a great way to give the humble spud the royal treatment and are very simple to make. Go on, give it a go!

INGREDIENTS

½ cup duck fat (or butter)
2 lb small to medium baking potatoes
Couple sprigs thyme
Salt
Cracked black pepper

NOTES:
You can also make this with bigger potatoes; you'll just need to roast them a bit longer or parboil them first.

If you can't get your hands on duck fat, use a combination of butter and olive oil, or even pork lard.

PREP

1. Preheat the oven to 350°F / 180°C.

METHOD

2. Melt the duck fat (or butter) in a roasting tray to the consistency of liquid, and pour out into a cup or jug.
3. Thinly slice potatoes two thirds of the way in, with evenly spaced slices. Place in the roasting tray, sliced side up.
4. Pour the duck fat over the potatoes, and brush the tops with the pastry brush.
5. Sprinkle with salt and pepper, and lay the sprigs of thyme on top.
6. Bake for 20 minutes in the middle of the oven, then brush the tops with butter or duck fat again by dipping the brush in the pan.
7. Bake for another 20 minutes or until tender and golden brown.

FINAL TOUCHES

8. Serve hot with your favorite Sunday roast.

Citrus & Honey Roasted Carrots SERVES 4–6

These sweet, earthy carrots are incredibly simple to make, and they go well with just about any dish imaginable. The slow-roasting process allows the interior to cook through gently, while the outside gets caramelized with that classic flavor combination of ginger and honey.

I love serving these with steak or as part of a large roast dinner.

EXTRA GEAR

Small roasting pan, just big enough to hold the carrots in a single layer

INGREDIENTS

- 10 oz small carrots
- 2 Tbsp honey
- ½ tsp minced ginger
- ¼ tsp cinnamon
- Salt, plus extra to season (use a nice finishing salt like Maldon if you can)

NOTES:
This technique works on carrots of all shapes and sizes. You will just need to adjust the amount of liquid used, as well as the cooking times. Smaller carrots (or large carrots cut into small pieces) will take much less time to cook.

PREP

1. Preheat oven to 285°F /140°C.
2. Wash the carrots. You can peel them if you want, but I prefer leaving the skin on.

METHOD

3. Place the carrots in the roasting pan.
4. Mix all the other ingredients together in the mixing bowl, and pour the mixture over the carrots.
5. Pop the pan in the oven, and roast the carrots until soft on the inside (test with a fork) and sticky and caramelized on the outside.
6. Check them every 30 minutes, turning them over as you go.

FINAL TOUCHES

7. Sprinkle some more salt on top for a bit of crunch.

Roasted Baby Beets with Arugula Yogurt

SERVES 6

Beets—people either love them or hate them. Personally, I fall squarely in the "Love them!" camp. My dad used to grow beets in his vegetable garden when I was a child and still does to this day.

Beets have a lovely earthy, sweet flavor. I prefer working with baby beets; they cook faster, and there's no need to peel them I've also recently discovered that honey and arugula go remarkably well together, so I decided to incorporate both in this dish. This is my new go-to recipe when I have to make something "salad-y."

EXTRA GEAR

Vegetable brush

INGREDIENTS

Beets

1½ lb of baby beets
4 cloves garlic, peeled
1 sprig of rosemary, cut in half
1 cup pecan nuts
Salt
Cracked black pepper

Sauce

Juice of 1 orange and 1 lemon (½ cup total)
2 Tbsp honey
2 Tbsp olive oil
1 Tbsp balsamic vinegar
Salt
Cracked black pepper

Yogurt

3 Tbsp plain double-thick yogurt
2 Tbsp chopped arugula leaves, plus extra for garnish
Zest of ½ lemon
2 tsp honey

PREP

1. Preheat oven to 350°F / 180°C.
2. Wash and trim the beets' stems to about ½ an inch long (you can cut them off completely if you wish, but I like leaving them on).
3. Mix all the ingredients for the sauce in a mixing bowl, and season with salt and pepper.

METHOD

4. Pop the beets, garlic, rosemary, and half the pecans in a roasting dish, and pour the sauce over. Toss the contents of the pan to coat everything in the sauce, and season with salt and pepper.
5. Tightly cover the pan with aluminum foil (shiny side down), and pop in the oven.
6. After 30 minutes, remove the foil, turn the beets over, and return to the oven.
7. Cook for 30–45 minutes longer, checking every 20 minutes or so for tenderness with a fork. It's up to you to decide how tender you want them. I prefer them soft, with just a little bit of bite left intact. Remove from the oven, and allow to cool to room temperature.
8. Mix the ingredients for the yogurt in a small mixing bowl.

9. Pop the other half of the pecans in a frying pan over medium heat, with a dash of olive oil and salt. Toast the nuts while tossing for about 1–2 minutes—be careful not to burn them.

FINAL TOUCHES

10. Transfer the beets to a serving dish or platter of your choice, and scatter dollops of yogurt across the dish.

11. Sprinkle the toasted pecans on top, then garnish with more chopped arugula.

Vanilla Ice Cream with "Cheats" Chocolate Sauce

MAKES 1.5 QUARTS OF ICE CREAM

Learning to make your own ice cream from scratch is a bit of a revelation. Once you realize you can make something this delicious at home at a fraction of the cost that premium brands or "artisanal producers" charge, you'll never spend top dollar on overpriced ice cream again.

It's simple, too, provided you buy yourself an ice cream churner. Just see it as an investment—it will pay for itself in no time. You can make a basic custard (flavored by whatever tickles your fancy), cool it down, churn it, and freeze it. Couldn't be simpler, right? And if you find yourself saying, "What do you mean 'just make a basic custard'? You don't know how often I burn the tea water," don't fear. Check out the recipe for homemade egg custard on page 246.

The fancy way of making a killer chocolate sauce is by melting ridiculously expensive chocolate (with a brand name you're never quite sure how to pronounce) over a double boiler, adding cream, and whisking until combined. That's all fine and well, but the problem is I never seem to have good chocolate in the house when I feel like making chocolate sauce.

This "cheats" version uses cheap ingredients that you probably have in the house already, and it can be knocked together in less than 30 minutes. Sure, the food snobs in your life (we all have them) might balk at the idea of using cocoa powder instead of real chocolate, but the vast majority of people you serve this to will be too busy licking their lips to concern themselves with such trivial matters. Do try to stay away from bulk cooking cocoa; instead, get the better-quality stuff, usually found in smaller tins. In short, use the best-quality cocoa you can afford.

EXTRA GEAR

Ice cream churner

INGREDIENTS

Ice cream

4 cups homemade egg custard (page 246)

Cheats Chocolate Sauce

1 cup good quality cocoa powder
1 cup sugar
2 cups water
1 Tbsp butter (optional)
½ tsp salt

Garnish

½ cup flaked almonds

PREP

1. Make the egg custard (page 246). Remove from heat, and allow to cool to room temperature. If you want to speed this up, pour the custard mix into a mixing bowl, and place on top of another mixing bowl filled with ice water. Refrigerate the mixture for 12 hours before churning; but if in a pinch, 3–4 hours will do the trick. The colder the mix is, the easier it will churn, especially with the churners that use "freezer bowls."
2. Churn the ice cream as per the manufacturer's instructions. (Basically, pour it into the churner, switch it on, and stop the machine when it's suitably thickened. At this stage, it will resemble soft serve.)
3. Freeze the ice cream for 4 hours before serving.

NOTES:
Most home churners come in two forms. The expensive models have cooling elements built in and thus are ready to churn at a moment's notice. The cheaper ones (like I have) use a bowl that you have to freeze up to 24 hours ahead of time. Both work perfectly fine. I typically leave my churner bowl in the freezer indefinitely; you never know when Ice Cream Fever might hit you.

METHOD

Chocolate sauce:

4. Add all the ingredients for the chocolate sauce except the butter to a large frying pan on medium heat, and whisk them together to combine. Once the mixture starts to boil, reduce the heat to a slow simmer, and let it cook for about 20 minutes, whisking the mixture every couple of minutes. At first it will be very watery, but have faith—soon the water will cook out, and you'll have a thick, gooey chocolate sauce.
5. You need to decide how thick you want the sauce to be, but bear in mind that the consistency will change drastically once the sauce hits the ice cream and cools down rapidly. If you make the sauce too thick in the pan, it will become rock-hard once cooled, and that's not what we are after. To test the consistency, drizzle some sauce on a cool plate. It will cool down quickly, and you'll have a good idea of what the actual consistency will be.
6. Once you hit the consistency you want, remove from heat, and whisk in the butter (optional).

FINAL TOUCHES

7. Put a dry nonstick frying pan on medium heat, and add the flaked almonds. Toast the almonds for a few minutes until they start to brown on the edges, then immediately transfer them to a cool bowl to stop the cooking. They go from toasted to burnt in a matter of seconds, so watch them like a hawk.
8. Serve the ice cream in your fanciest bowls, drizzle a scandalous amount of sauce on top, and sprinkle with the toasted almonds.

Love Your Leftovers

Bread & Butter Pudding

SERVES 6

I love sourdough bread and can't resist buying a loaf (or three) when walking past them in a bakery, which inevitably leads to me having way too much bread at home and some of it going stale.

You could freeze the bread to preserve its freshness, I suppose, but who wants to freeze things when you can make this bread and butter pudding instead? Bread that is somewhat stale is perfect for bread and butter pudding, which is friggin' delicious. I rest my case.

INGREDIENTS

Custard

- 1 vanilla bean
- 2 cups milk
- 4 eggs
- ½ cup cream
- 2 oranges, zested
- pinch of ground nutmeg
- 1½ tsp cinnamon
- 1 tsp almond essence
- ½ tsp salt

The rest

- 1 loaf any white bread
- ½ cup butter, plus extra to grease your baking dish
- ½ cup apricot jam, plus 2 Tbsp extra for glazing
- ½ cup chocolate chips
- ½ cup flaked almonds

NOTES:
To learn more about working with real vanilla beans, see page 12.

PREP

1. Preheat the oven to 340°C / 170°C.
2. Split the vanilla bean in half lengthways with a paring knife, and scrape out the seeds with the back of the knife. Discard the empty husk.
3. Whisk all the ingredients for the custard together.
4. Slice the bread, and spread generously with butter and jam. Butter your baking dish evenly.

METHOD

5. Pack a layer of half of the bread slices into your dish, and sprinkle with chocolate chips. Pour enough custard mix in to cover the bread, and you'll see it start to soak in. Add another layer of bread, and top with the remaining custard mix, chocolate chips, and almonds.
6. Bake for around 30 minutes in the middle of the oven. To check if it is baked, gently tip the dish to see if unbaked custard dribbles out. If not, you are ready to go.

FINAL TOUCHES

7. Mix the extra apricot jam with a bit of warm water, and glaze the top of the pudding with a pastry brush. Serve right away with vanilla ice cream or lashings of whipped cream.

Fried Polenta SERVES 4

Leftover polenta can be reheated with a little milk and a whole lot of whisking, but the texture is never quite the same.

Fried polenta is an excellent way to give leftover polenta a second chance to shine. Paired with a Bloody Mary sauce, this quick and easy meal will help sort out that hangover you inherited after a night of abundant red wine and osso buco on polenta (see page 169).

INGREDIENTS

Cooked polenta, warmed
Neutral oil
Couple sprigs thyme
Parmesan, or other Italian hard cheese

Bloody Mary dipping sauce

1 cup tomato juice
2 tsp lemon juice
1 tsp Worcestershire sauce
1 tsp Sriracha (or other hot sauce)
Pinch of sugar
Shot of vodka (optional)
½ tsp salt
½ tsp cracked black pepper

PREP

1. The polenta should still be warm and pourable. If you slipped up and the polenta has gone solid, heat it up with a little milk or water and stir vigorously until you have pourable polenta again.

2. Oil a baking dish that will hold the amount of polenta you have on hand so it lays about ½ inch thick. Flatten it out with a spatula or by shaking the dish. Let it cool to room temperature, then chill in the fridge for at least an hour or overnight.

3. Before you cook, mix all the ingredients for the Bloody Mary dipping sauce together, and taste and adjust the seasoning to your liking.

METHOD

4. To remove the polenta, place a cutting board on top of the dish and flip it over, holding the board and dish together with both hands. Wiggle the dish, and the slab of polenta should pop right out. Cut off the rounded edges to make the slab perfectly square, then slice into batons ½ inch thick.

5. Add oil to a frying pan so it comes up to a height of a ½ inch. Heat the oil to just before smoking. Strip off some thyme leaves, and add to the oil.

6. Shallow fry the batons in batches of five for about 3–4 minutes on all sides until golden and crispy. Remove from oil, and drain on paper towels.

7. Lay out the batons on a serving plate, and let it rain with grated Parmesan using a grater. Roll the batons in the cheese so they are coated on all sides.

FINAL TOUCHES

8. Pour the Bloody Mary sauce into small dipping bowls.

9. Grate a little more Parmesan over the polenta batons, and enjoy.

Steak Sandwich SERVES 2

There is a reason why I always end up with at least one extra steak when I've had people over for a *braai* (that's the Afrikaans word everyone in South Africa uses for an outdoor grilling session).

It's not because I miscalculate the steak-per-guest ratio every single time. It's not because I have managed to convert my vegan girlfriend into developing a fondness for fine quality beef.

Nope, the reason, gentlemen, is steak sandwiches. Read on.

EXTRA GEAR

Griddle pan
Skewer (optional)

INGREDIENTS

8 oz cooked steak
4 medium pickles
Couple slices Emmental cheese (or your favorite type)
4 slices sourdough bread (or any other of good quality)
Olive oil
½ cup packed arugula leaves
Salt
Cracked black pepper

Sauce

2 Tbsp mayonnaise
1 Tbsp wholegrain mustard
1 tsp honey
1 Tbsp plain double thick yogurt

PREP

1. Slice the steak, pickles, and cheese.
2. Add the mayonnaise, mustard, honey, and yogurt to a cup, and mix well.

METHOD

3. Put the griddle pan on medium high heat. Drizzle the bread with olive oil and arrange in the pan. Turn after 1 minute, and cook for another minute on the other side. Remove bread from the pan, and allow to cool.
4. When the toast has cooled to warm, start building this bad boy. Put a slice of bread on a plate, spread a layer of sauce, and scatter arugula leaves on top.
5. Add the steak, pickle, and cheese on top, and season with a little salt and pepper. Drizzle more sauce over, and cover with the other slice of bread.

FINAL TOUCHES

6. Gently lay your hand on top of the sandwich and slice it through (the sandwich, not your hand). Stack the two halves on top of each other, and drive a skewer through the top to keep the stack stable.
7. Grab a good beer, sit back, and enjoy.

Carbonara Omelet

SERVES 1

So, let's say you find yourself with some leftover cooked spaghetti, but zero sauce. What is a man to do? Slap together a carbonara omelet, of course! This recipe is pretty much the exact opposite of how you'd make a decent, authentic spaghetti carbonara (see page 187). The spaghetti makes the omelet more filling, removing the need for toast on the side. The idea may sound weird, but give it a try.

INGREDIENTS

- 1 cup pecorino or Parmesan (plus extra to garnish)
- 3 eggs
- 4 rashers of bacon
- 2 tsp olive oil
- Cooked spaghetti
- Salt
- Cracked black pepper
- 2 tsp butter

NOTES:
If you do happen to have guanciale (Italian cured pork jowl) on hand (or know where to get some), use it. Its flavor is worth a little extra effort.

PREP

1. Grate the cheese, and divide into two portions. Whisk the eggs and half of the cheese in a small bowl.

2. Slice the bacon into lardons (short, small strips).

METHOD

3. Heat olive oil in the pan on medium-high heat. Fry the bacon until crispy, then remove from pan. Add the spaghetti to the pan, and fry for a minute or so. Cold spaghetti clumps together, so gently work the noodles apart with tongs.

4. Pour the egg mixture into the pan, and keep shaking things up with the tongs, creating openings so the uncooked egg can reach the bottom of the pan. After 20 seconds or so, the egg will start to solidify. Arrange the bacon and cheese into one half of the omelet. Season with salt and pepper.

5. Using the spatula, flip the empty half of the omelet over the bacon and cheese. Don't fret too much if it tears; we'll hide it later. Add the butter and tilt the pan toward the omelet. Lift the omelet just a little so the butter can move underneath, then put the pan down and let it fry for 20 seconds or so.

6. Remove the pan from heat, and tilt it down away from you so the omelet lies in the bottom part of the pan. Gently tap it against a cutting board to help it along if needed. Tilt the omelet out onto a plate so that the side that was fried in butter is on top. If you want to change your grip on the pan to make this easier, grip the handle with your thumb pointing away from the pan, allowing you to tilt the pan without weird arm movements.

FINAL TOUCHES

7. Grate a little more cheese on top, and sprinkle with freshly cracked black pepper.

Salmon Fish Cakes

SERVES 6

Fish cakes are made in different variations the world over. Initially meant as a way of using up leftover fish and potatoes, these days you get rather fancy versions (like this one) that use expensive ingredients like salmon for a marked difference in flavor.

Kick things up a notch by making your own tartar sauce, buy some if you are in a particularly lazy mood, or just slap mayonnaise on there if you really can't be bothered.

INGREDIENTS

Fish Cakes

⁴⁄₅ lb medium potatoes (waxy)
1 cup chopped parsley
Zest and juice of 1 lemon
2 Tbsp breadcrumbs (optional, to make a thicker cake)
5½ Tbsp / 3 oz good quality ketchup
Salt
Cracked black pepper
³⁄₅ lb cooked salmon
3 Tbsp neutral oil

Tartar sauce

1 pickled cucumber
10 capers
2 Tbsp mayonnaise
1 Tbsp horseradish sauce
1 lemons juice and zest
1 tsp white wine vinegar
Salt
Cracked black pepper

PREP

1. Peel, quarter, and boil your potatoes in salted water.
2. Drain, and allow to cool for 15 minutes.

NOTES:
These fish cakes freeze well for up to 2 months, so make a large batch, and freeze the rest for an easy weekday meal.

METHOD

3. In a large mixing bowl, mash your potatoes, but not to a smooth paste.
4. Add the rest of the ingredients except the salmon and oil, and mix well. Taste your mix, and add more salt if you wish.
5. Flake your salmon into the bowl, and gently incorporate. The mixture should be chunky rather than mashed.
6. Add a little oil to a small frying pan, and bring to a shimmer over a medium-high heat. Once the oil is hot enough to sizzle, add the fishcakes to the pan. If you add them to not-quite-hot-enough oil, the fishcake will soak up too much oil and become soggy.
7. Fry each fishcake for around 1–2 minutes on each side until golden.
8. Remove from the pan and set onto paper towels to drain. Salt immediately.

FINAL TOUCHES

9. For the tartar sauce, finely dice the pickle and capers, and add to a bowl with the rest of the ingredients. Mix, and add more salt and pepper if you wish.

Short Rib & Jalapeño Croquettes SERVES 4–6

Croquettes are one of those things that taste way better than you think they would, especially judging by what it costs you to make them.

Traditionally made as a way to use up leftovers, croquettes are so damn good you may soon find yourself cooking large quantities of meat for no particularly reason other than to make another batch of these bad boys.

Croquettes are a great way to experiment with different flavor combinations. I used beef short rib here, but the recipe can be tweaked to use any meat, seafood, or vegetables. Just adapt the herbs and spices as needed to complement the type of meat used. You really can't go too wrong here, but keep the ratio of meat to white sauce in check.

EXTRA GEAR

Rubber spatula
Oil thermometer

INGREDIENTS

Meat

1 lb cooked beef short rib
1 medium onion
3 cloves garlic
4 medium jalapeño chilies
1 Tbsp olive oil
1 tsp dried Italian herb mix
1 Tbsp Worcestershire sauce
Salt
Cracked black pepper

White sauce (see page 21, using ingredients listed below)

3 Tbsp butter
½ cup bread flour
2 cups milk
Pinch of nutmeg
Salt
Cracked black pepper

Croquettes

4 Tbsp flour (with extra to dust)
4 eggs, whisked
2 cups breadcrumbs
Oil, enough for five inches deep in a pan for frying

NOTES:
I love making big batches of these and freezing them just before the frying step. They are quite a mission to make, so while you're at it, you might as well keep going and make extra for those nights when you crave them but don't feel like the hassle.

PREP

1. Chop the meat up finely. Exactly how fine is up to you, but if you leave the pieces too chunky, you'll have trouble forming the croquettes.

2. Dice the onion, garlic, and jalapeños—again, not too chunky.

METHOD

3. Add olive oil to the pan, and put it on medium heat. Fry the onion, garlic, and jalapenos for 2–3 minutes.

4. Add the meat, dried herbs, and Worcestershire sauce to the pan, and stir through. Fry for 2–3 minutes, then have a taste and adjust seasoning as needed.

5. Remove the meat and veggies from the pan. Start making the white sauce in the same pan.

6. Prepare the white sauce (page 21), using the ingredients listed above. This will make a thicker sauce for the croquettes..

7. Add the meat and veggies back into the pan with the sauce, and mix through. Have a taste again, and adjust seasoning as needed.

8. Pour the mixture out of the pan into a rectangular container, spreading the mix out evenly, about an inch high. Allow to cool to room temperature, then pop in the fridge for an hour or two to set.

9. Using a spatula, cut the croquette base into rectangles, and 2½ inches long. Gently roll these into round logs, and dust with flour.

10. Now, for the breading. Get an assembly line setup going with three dinner bowls. The first should contain flour, the second whisked eggs, and the third breadcrumbs.

11. Dredge the croquettes in flour, then egg, then breadcrumbs, shaking off the excess as you go. Repeat this process twice for each log, so you are basically double-breading them.

12. Pop the croquettes in the fridge to firm up while you get the oil ready. Add enough oil to the pot so it's roughly 5 inches deep, and put it on medium heat. You want the oil between 320°F and 350°F (160°C and 180°C).

13. Fry the croquettes two or three at a time until golden brown and crispy. Remove from the oil, and drain on paper towels. Sprinkle a little salt on the croquettes while hot. The salt will stick to the surface oil and get absorbed.

FINAL TOUCHES

14. Serve the croquettes with ketchup or hot mustard.

Feeding a Crowd

Osso Buco with Polenta SERVES 6–8

Osso buco, translated as *bone with a hole* or *hollow bone*, is an Italian classic—comfort food at its best. It's one of those things you just want to eat more of, even though "you really shouldn't." I love serving it on buttery polenta, but risotto or mashed potatoes work great, too.

It may look like a lengthy recipe, but please don't let that scare you off. It's really not difficult; it just takes a little time, like most good things do.

Gremolata is the secret ingredient in this dish, and its importance cannot be overstated. It supplies a fresh, zingy kick that cuts through the rich, meaty stew and lifts up the whole shebang to next-level goodness. Try it out; you'll see what I mean.

EXTRA GEAR

Kitchen twine
Large hob and oven-safe casserole or Dutch oven

INGREDIENTS

Osso buco

1 medium onion
2 medium carrots
1 stick celery
3 cloves garlic
Big handful fresh Italian herbs (basil, thyme, rosemary, oregano, etc.)
½ cup all-purpose flour
Salt
Cracked black pepper
3–4 lb veal shank, cross-cut into 1½–2-inch slices
3 Tbsp olive oil
½ cup tomato paste
1 cup dry white wine
1 14-oz can whole peeled tomatoes
2–3 bay leaves
2 cups chicken stock
Knob of butter

Polenta

1 tsp salt
4 cups water
1 cup polenta
3 Tbsp butter
½ cup grated Parmesan or pecorino (or more)

Gremolata

1 large handful flat leaf parsley
3 cloves garlic, chopped
1 lemon
Olive oil, to drizzle

NOTES:

If you can't find veal shank, beef shank can be used as a substitute. You'll need to cook it longer, as beef is quite a bit tougher.

If you burn the pan while frying the meat, stop and clean it out before adding the vegetables. You do want browned bits in the pan (that's basically meat candy right there), but burned black bits will impart a bitter flavor.

PREP

1. Preheat the oven to 320°F / 160°C.

2. Dice the onions, carrots, celery, and garlic. Aim for equally sized pieces so they will cook evenly. Tie the fresh herbs together with kitchen twine.

METHOD

Osso Buco:

3. Add the flour, salt, and pepper to a mixing bowl, and mix through. Dredge the slices of meat in the flour, and set aside.

4. Add olive oil to your casserole or Dutch oven. Brown the meat in batches, and set aside on a separate plate as you go. Do not overcrowd the pan. It's essential that you get good color on the meat, so take your time. In cooking, color equals flavor. Doing it right will enhance the overall flavor of the dish like you wouldn't believe.

5. When the meat is browned, remove it. Add diced onions, carrots, and celery to the empty pan, and fry for 4–5 minutes until you see some color developing. Add the tomato paste, and cook it out for 2–3 minutes.

6. Deglaze the pan (see page 25) by adding a dash of white wine and scraping off the browned bits on the bottom of the pan with a wooden spoon. We want that stuff in the sauce.

7. Add the garlic, herbs, tomatoes, bay leaves, and chicken stock, and bring it all to a low simmer. Taste the sauce, and adjust seasoning as needed.

8. Add the meat back into the pan, pop the lid on, and stick it in the oven for 1½–2 hours. Check it every 30 minutes after the first hour. Actual cooking time may vary depending on the meat used. When it is ready, you'll be able to push the meat off the bone with a spoon (don't do that, though; keeping the bone in is the best part).

Polenta:

9. Add salt to the water, and bring to a boil. Slowly add the polenta while stirring. Turn the heat down to a low simmer, and put the lid on.

10. Let it simmer for 40 minutes, checking every 10 minutes or so to make sure it hasn't developed clumps and isn't sticking to the bottom of the pan. Keep the temperature low and the lid on so you don't lose too much moisture. Check and stir every 5 minutes after an initial 20 minutes, and add more water if things get too dry.

11. You will see the polenta start to pull away from the edges of the pot and develop a creamier texture when it's ready. Remove from the heat, add the butter and cheese, and stir through.

Gremolata:

12. Place the parsley, garlic, and lemon zest on a cutting board, and drizzle olive oil over it

13. Start chopping everything up, mixing as you go. Some people like the ingredients chopped fine; I prefer mine chunkier. Your call.

14. Scrape the mix off the board and into a small bowl.

FINAL TOUCHES

15. To serve, add a generous helping of polenta in the center of a plate. Top with a piece of meat and some extra sauce drizzled over. Garnish with dots of gremolata all over, and dig in!

Sweet Potato Flatbreads with Zucchini & Ricotta

SERVES 4–6

Nine times out of ten, the simplest recipes are the best ones. Take this sweet potato flatbread (roti), for example. The flatbread itself has two ingredients: sweet potato and flour. Yup, that's it. They are also incredibly versatile and can be matched with sweet or savory toppings.

My girlfriend, Claire, is vegan (yeah, meat lovers and vegans can get along just fine, who'd have thunk?), so we wanted to include a vegan recipe in this book. I was skeptical at first (I have deliciousness standards to uphold, ya know), but the second I bit into one of these, I quickly changed my mind. In the end, I added some ricotta to mine, just to balance out the vegan-ness a bit; one can never be too careful.

I still can't quite figure out how just four ingredients can combine to become something this delicious, but they do, so trust me, and knock together a batch of these. You'll thank me later.

EXTRA GEAR

Griddle pan
Rolling pin
Steaming basket or small colander

INGREDIENTS

1 cup steamed sweet potato
4 medium sized zucchini
Salt
Cracked black pepper
Neutral oil (like canola)
1 cup all-purpose flour (and extra for dusting)
1 jar (about 5 oz) basil pesto
½ cup (packed) basil leaves
150–200g Ricotta
1 cup olives

PREP

1. Peel and cube the sweet potato. Steam in a steaming basket (or small colander) above boiling water in a pot with the lid on for about 15–20 minutes until soft. Set aside and allow to cool.

2. Cut the ends off the zucchini, and slice into thin ribbons. Season with salt and pepper, and drizzle with a dash of neutral oil.

METHOD

3. Heat the griddle pan and fry the zucchini ribbons for roughly one minute a side until charred lines are formed.

4. Combine the sweet potato and flour to form a firm dough. Divide the dough into small balls just a little bigger than a golf ball.

5. On a floured work surface, roll the balls out nice and thin with a rolling pin (about ⅒ inch should do). Turn them as you roll them out to keep them round(ish).

6. Heat a nonstick frying pan on medium-high heat, and add about a teaspoon of neutral oil. Add a flatbread and cook 1½ minutes on one side, then flip and cook another minute on the other side. Repeat with the rest of the balls. Drain the flatbread on paper towels, and salt each one lightly.

7. Spread a generous layer of pesto over the flatbreads, then add the rest of the toppings.

FINAL TOUCHES

8. Season with a little more salt and black pepper, and serve.

Tomato & Feta Pull-Apart Rolls SERVES 6–8

These rolls are great for parties. Because they are prefilled and pulled apart by your guests, you don't have to worry about them being shaped perfectly or about some of your guests hogging all the toppings, leaving the rest with dry rolls and less-than-friendly facial expressions.

This recipe is easily adaptable, so mix things up with the fillings, and come up with your own favorite combination. Think bacon and cheese, spinach and feta, ham and mushroom—you get the idea.

Rolling up the dough can be slightly tricky for one person to do, so best to get a friend along for the ride and blame everything on them if the rolls don't turn out as expected.

EXTRA GEAR

Large work surface
Rolling pin
Pastry brush

INGREDIENTS

½ cup olive oil
Flour, to dust
2 lb bread dough
1 14-oz can tomato and onion mix
2 Tbsp Sriracha
Salt
Cracked black pepper
5 oz cherry tomatoes
10 oz feta cheese
4 oz mozzarella cheese
4 oz basil pesto
15 basil leaves

NOTES:
You can buy ready-made bread dough from your bakery or grocery store, or make it yourself (see page 247).

PREP

1. Preheat oven to 340°F / 170°C.

METHOD

2. Pour 2 Tbsp of olive oil into the dish and spread it around, making sure to grease the bottom as well as the sides of the dish.

3. On a floured surface, roll out the bread dough into a large rectangle using a rolling pin, about a quarter inch thick.

4. Mix the tomato and onion mix, Sriracha, and a generous pinch of salt and pepper. Spread out on the dough with a spatula.

5. Slice the cherry tomatoes, and arrange them evenly on the dough. Crumble the feta, and grate the mozzarella evenly over the dough. Scatter dots of pesto and basil leaves all over.

6. Tightly roll up the dough, pinching it down as you go. Try to pull it as tight as you can without tearing the dough. Cut the rolled-up dough into pieces 2½ inches wide, and arrange in the baking dish.

7. Brush lightly with 2 Tbsp of olive oil, and leave in warm place to proof (see page 252) for 20–30 minutes at room temperature, or until it has increased its original size by half. You may need to let it proof a little longer in cold weather.

8. Bake in the middle of the oven for 25 minutes, or until golden brown.

FINAL TOUCHES

9. Brush with the remaining 4 Tbsp of olive oil, and season with salt and pepper.

Roasted Smashed Baby Potatoes with Garlic

SERVES 6–8

Why would you smash up a perfectly good potato, you may ask? Well, there is method to this madness.

When you smash the potato, you open up cracks, exposing the potato to the heat and oil. That means more of its surface area will crisp up and brown, resulting in a crispier and more flavorful roasted potato.

EXTRA GEAR

Roasting pan
Pastry brush

INGREDIENTS

1½ lb baby potatoes
4 Tbsp olive oil
1 head of garlic
Salt
Cracked black pepper

PREP

1. Preheat the oven to 350°F / 180°C.

2. Boil baby potatoes for around 10–15 minutes, depending on the size of your potatoes.

METHOD

3. Add olive oil to a roasting pan. Slice the whole head of garlic in half, and add it to the pan.

4. Add your baby potatoes, and, with your thumb, lightly squash them to break the skin open.

5. Sprinkle with salt and pepper. Brush the potatoes with the oil in the pan to coat.

6. Roast on the top shelf of the oven for 15 minutes, then turn your potatoes and roast for another 15 minutes or until the skins are golden and your garlic is soft.

FINAL TOUCHES

7. Serve just like that in the roasting pan, and let your guests help themselves.

Lamb Neck & Vegetable Soup

SERVES 6–8

This recipe has been a winter staple in our family since I can remember, so when I moved out of the house to go to college, I persuaded my dad to hand over the recipe.

There is nothing complex about it, and no fancy techniques—it is really simple to make. If you can't find lamb knuckle, you can substitute it with beef or pork (though the original is best).

My dad's recipe contained a pack of vegetable instant soup mix, one of those "just add water" jobs, but I prefer making things from scratch, so I have tweaked it in my recipe.

EXTRA GEAR

6-quart pot
Soup ladle

INGREDIENTS

2 lb lamb neck
2 large potatoes
3 large carrots
2 medium onions
2 lb cabbage
2 Tbsp olive oil
Salt
1 tsp dried oregano
1 tsp dried basil
1 tsp dried thyme
2 tsp Worcestershire sauce
Cracked black pepper
2 Tbsp corn flour

PREP

1. Cut the lamb neck in half lengthwise, and then slice into 1½-inch pieces.

2. Grate the potatoes and carrots, and add to a large mixing bowl. I prefer keeping the skin on for more flavor and nutrients, but you can peel them if you wish. Roughly chop the onions, and add them to the bowl. Slice the cabbage into thin slivers, and add to the bowl.

METHOD

3. Pop the pot on medium-high heat, and add the olive oil. Once it starts shimmering, fry the meat until browned, and set aside. Do this in batches.

4. Once all the meat is browned, add it back to the pot, and cover with 2 inches of water. Bring the water up to a boil, then reduce the heat to a gentle simmer. Add a generous helping of salt; about 1 tablespoon should do it. That might seem excessive, but the soup

NOTES:

The only important part in this recipe is the order in which you add the ingredients. The meat needs to cook until tender before you start adding vegetables, otherwise the veggies will cook to smithereens by the time the meat is ready.

Remember that adding more water will dilute the seasoning, but the reverse is also true. The more you cook the soup, the more it'll steam off the water, reducing the amount of liquid. For that reason, you should never add the total amount of seasoning up front, but rather taste and adjust as you go, leaving the final adjustment for just before serving.

contains a lot of water that dilutes the seasoning. Simmer with a lid on for 90 minutes, stirring things around every 30 minutes and scooping off the foam that accumulates on top of the water with a spoon.

5. Once the meat has been cooking for 90 minutes, it will start to separate from the bones. Add the bowl of mixed cut vegetables, herbs (oregano, basil, and thyme), Worcestershire sauce, and a generous pinch or two of pepper, and cook for another 20 minutes.

6. In a separate bowl, mix the corn flour with a little bit of water, stirring until it forms a smooth paste. Add the paste to the pot and stir through. Turn the heat down to a low simmer, and cook for another 2–3 minutes. Taste the soup, and adjust seasoning if needed.

FINAL TOUCHES

7. Serve the soup steaming hot with some crusty bread, and you'll have yourself a meal fit for a king.

Spaghetti & Meatballs SERVES 4

Who doesn't love a big ol' plate of spaghetti and meatballs? In my opinion, the secret is in the tomato sauce. It is possible to make a quick tomato sauce, but cooking it low and slow allows the tomatoes to break down, become sweeter, and develop a much deeper flavor.

Making the oven do most of the work saves a lot of effort. You can quickly slap the sauce together, then let it simmer in the oven for hours while you take care of the rather serious business of relaxing after a hard day's work. Later, when you are ready to eat. you can make the meatballs and spaghetti in less than 30 minutes.

The sauce also freezes well, so feel free to make double the quantity and freeze half of it for even less effort the next time you need to throw together a tomato-based dish—think lasagna, cannelloni, etc.

EXTRA GEAR

Colander

INGREDIENTS

Sauce

1 medium yellow onion
2 medium carrots
1 rib celery
4 cloves garlic
5 Tbsp olive oil, plus extra for frying
4 oz tomato paste
1 cup water
2 28-oz tins chopped tomatoes
2 tsp sugar
1 Tbsp Worcestershire sauce

Meatballs

1 medium yellow onion
½ cup chopped flat leaf parsley
1 lb / 450 g ground beef
1 lb / 450 g ground pork
2 tsp kosher salt
1 tsp cracked black pepper
1 cup coarse breadcrumbs (with a little more to spare)
2 eggs
2 tsp Worcestershire sauce

Spaghetti

1 lb pack spaghetti
Salt

Garnish

Hunk hard Italian cheese (like Parmesan)
Handful basil leaves, sliced into thin shreds

NOTES:

If you don't have an oven, you can also simmer the tomato sauce low and slow on the stove top. Just check the moisture levels and add water as needed, and stir—a lot. The oven works better because the pot gets heat from all sides, and since the heat is less intense, there is no need for constant stirring.

PREP

Sauce:

1. The sauce takes the longest, so let's hit that first. Preheat the oven to 300°F / 150°C.

2. Peel and dice the onion. Grate the carrots. Slice the celery into roughly ¼-inch slices. Mince the garlic.

3. Bring a Dutch oven up to medium-high heat on the stove, and add 2 Tbsp olive oil. Fry the onion, carrot, and celery for 3–4 minutes, then add the garlic, and cook for a further 3 minutes.

4. Make a clearing in the middle of the pot with a spoon, and add 1 Tbsp of oil. Pop the tomato paste in, and stir with a wooden spoon to combine with the oil. Fry the paste until it turns dark red, about 2–3 minutes. Caramelizing the paste brings a lot more depth to the tomato flavor in your sauce.

5. Deglaze the pan with a splash of water (see page 25), then add the rest of the water, as well as the tomatoes, sugar, and Worcestershire sauce. Stir through, and bring to a boil.

6. Transfer the pot to the oven. Let it reduce and caramelize for 3 hours, stirring every hour or so.

METHOD

Meatballs:

7. Peel and finely dice the onion. Roughly chop the parsley.

8. Add the meat to a large mixing bowl. Try spreading the meat out as much as you can by gently breaking it up with your fingers; do not squash it. Season with salt and pepper, spreading the seasoning evenly over the meat.

9. Add the onion, parsley, and breadcrumbs, then whisk the eggs with a fork and add them, too. Gently combine the mixture with your hands. Don't overwork it; you just want to mix it through. If the mixture feels too wet, add a little more breadcrumbs (but don't overdo it).

10. Fill a small bowl with water, and form meatballs in the size you want them, wetting your hands every now and then to prevent sticking. Place the meatballs on a cookie sheet or tray, and cover with cling wrap until ready to cook.

11. Heat about 2 Tbsp of olive oil in a pan over medium-high heat, and fry the meatballs in batches. You just want to brown them on all sides, not cook them through. We will finish them off in the sauce.

12. When the meatballs are browned, add them to the sauce that is bubbling away in the oven, and let them simmer for 15–20 minutes until cooked. Remove the meatballs from the sauce, and set aside.

Spaghetti:

13. Get a large pot of salted water going on high heat. Read the instructions on the back of the pasta packet. Take note of the suggested cooking time, and subtract 2 minutes. Add the pasta to the pot, and gently stir until the pasta is covered with water. When the pasta has finished cooking for the modified cooking time, drain in a colander. Do not rinse it!

14. Put the pasta back into the pasta pot, and add the tomato sauce. Use tongs to mix things up, making sure to coat the spaghetti with sauce.

15. Transfer the pasta and tomato sauce to a serving dish, and pop the meatballs on top. Pop the dish in the oven for 5–10 minutes to get everything piping hot before serving.

FINAL TOUCHES

16. Garnish with shredded fresh basil and some grated Parmesan cheese.

Date Night

Spaghetti Carbonara

SERVES 2–4

I was first introduced to the beauty of this dish and Italian cooking by a good friend, Mario Piazza, a warm-blooded Italian scoundrel. At the time, I knew very little about cooking, and I was fascinated when he managed to create such a tasty dish in so little time with so few ingredients. I believe this was when my love affair with Italian food really got going.

The beauty of spaghetti carbonara lies in its simplicity. Because we are using just a handful of ingredients, it's the perfect time to let them shine. You'll be richly rewarded for going through the extra trouble (and/or expense) of buying the best ingredients you can get your hands on, as opposed to the cheap and nasty stuff you'll find at the corner store.

INGREDIENTS

Salt, for boiling water
½ lb guanciale, pancetta, or bacon
Dash of oil
3 eggs + 3 extra yolks (to separate eggs, see page 37)
1½ cup freshly grated Parmesan, pecorino, or a mixture of the two (plus extra to serve)
Cracked black pepper
1 pack dried spaghetti (or other pasta of your choice)

NOTES:

CAUTION: While the eggs in the sauce do get cooked by the residual heat left in the pasta, there is always a chance of some raw egg staying around. I prefer it that way, but babies or anyone with a compromised immune system may want to avoid this dish. Best bet is to let your guests decide.

Traditionally, guanciale (cured pork cheek) is used in this recipe. Do your best to get your hands on some—trust me, it's worth it. If you really can't find any guanciale, go for pancetta. If you can't find either of those, you can settle for bacon.

When it comes to the cheese, buy a block of hard Italian cheese, and grate it yourself. Forget about using that powdery, white, lifeless stuff from a shaker that people call Parmesan. Get real cheese.

Warm-blooded Italians are prone to engage in heated debates as to whether Parmesan or pecorino should be used. Truth be told, either of them or a mix of the two will work just fine.

PREP

1. Fill a big pot with water, and bring to a boil. Add salt as required—about ¾ to 1 tablespoon of fine sea salt per quart/liter should be a good guideline (I normally just eyeball it). Bear in mind that very little of the salt actually sticks to the pasta; most of it goes down the drain with the pasta water. Play around with water-to-salt ratios, and find what works for you. Do not add oil to the pasta water to prevent sticking—it doesn't help.

2. Cut the guanciale into cubes or small strips—entirely your preference.

METHOD

3. Add a dash of olive oil to a pan on medium-low heat. Once it has heated up, add the guanciale. We want to render some of the fat out of the meat fairly slowly, so keep an eye on it, and move the meat around while it cooks. It should be nice and crispy, but not burnt. Remove the pan from the heat when done.

4. Add the eggs (whole eggs plus the extra yolks), cheese, and black pepper to a mixing bowl, and whisk together.

5. By now your pasta water should have reached a rolling boil. Drop in the pasta. After 2 minutes, use tongs to stir through and loosen up the pasta to prevent the strands from sticking to the bottom of the pot or one another. Cooking time will vary, so I start testing after 8 minutes by biting into a strand. Check every minute or so until the pasta is al dente.

6. Using a cup, scoop up some pasta water and set aside—you will need it to adjust the consistency of the sauce.

7. Drain the pasta, and pop it into the mixing bowl with the cheese. Immediately start to stir it well with the tongs. The heat from the pasta will start cooking the eggs, coating the pasta as it goes. Once the sauce starts to stiffen up, add a little pasta water, as well as the contents from the guanciale pan. If you are on a low-fat diet, pour out most of the fat before doing so.

8. Keep, stirring, lifting, and dropping the pasta in the bowl with the tongs. If it stiffens up, add another splash of pasta water; if it gets too runny, pop the entire contents back into the pan (or pot) on the stove and heat it up over gentle heat while stirring.

FINAL TOUCHES

9. To serve, grate more cheese on top, and sprinkle generously with black pepper.

Pan-Fried Salmon with Dill Potatoes SERVES 2

Salmon is hellishly expensive in my part of the world, but when it comes to special occasions (like a date night), I like to pull out all the stops and frown at the bills later. Life is too short to not eat the best food you can get your hands on once in a while.

Salmon with dill potatoes is a classic Scandinavian combination. I've been to Sweden twice, and you see it on menus everywhere—and it's always marvelous.

You can make the dill potatoes ahead of time and just fry the fish before serving, making this a great dish for entertaining that special someone.

INGREDIENTS

Dill potatoes

Salt, for boiling water
10 baby potatoes
1 cup dill
1 Tbsp capers
1 cup crème fraîche
1 lemons, zested and juiced
2 small spring onions, thinly sliced
¼ cup fresh fennel bulb, shaved (with a knife or a mandolin)
¼ small yellow onion, finely diced
Cracked black pepper

Salmon

2 salmon steaks
Salt
Cracked black pepper
1 Tbsp fresh dill
1 Tbsp neutral oil
1 small lemon

NOTES:
If you can't find crème fraîche, use sour cream, and whisk in a tablespoon of heavy cream to thin it out a little.

PREP

Dill potatoes:

1. Fill a pot of salted water, and boil the baby potatoes for around 15 minutes. Drain, and allow to cool.

2. Chop the dill and capers, and add to a small mixing bowl along with the crème fraîche, lemon, salt, and pepper. Chill in the fridge for 15 minutes to firm up.

3. Once the potatoes have cooled, slice them in half. In a large mixing bowl, combine the baby potatoes, crème fraîche mix, and the rest of the potato salad ingredients.

4. Set in the fridge to cool.

METHOD

Salmon:

5. Pat the salmon fillets dry with kitchen towels. Chop the dill.

6. Using a very sharp knife, score the skin by gently squeezing the skin together with your thumb and forefinger, and make 5 shallow cuts across the skin, only just piercing the flesh. You do this to prevent the skin from retracting and causing your fish to curl up when cooking. Grind salt and pepper onto the skins, and sprinkle with chopped dill.

7. In a medium-sized pan, heat oil over medium-high heat. Once heated, add one piece of fish, skin-side down. It should sizzle immediately. If you don't hear the sizzle, the oil is too cold. Remove the fish, and try again after a minute.

8. Leave to cook for 1½ minutes. You will see the orange flesh turning whiter along the sides at the bottom. Using a spatula, gently lift a corner of the fish to view the progress of the cooking skin. It should look golden brown and crispy. Turn your salmon and cook for another minute, depending on the thickness of your fish.

9. The majority of the fish should turn white on the sides. You really don't want to overcook the salmon, so err on the side of taking it out too soon. You can always pop it back in the pan if need be, but you can't undo overcooking. People eat salmon raw in sushi all the time, so don't stress. Press the salmon with your fingers to judge doneness—it should feel firm, but also like it could give way if you pushed too hard.

FINAL TOUCHES

10. Slice two cheeks of lemon, and fry skin-side up in the oil from the fish pan.

11. Spoon the potato salad onto two plates, and place your salmon fillet on top. Serve with the blackened lemon cheeks.

Mussels in White Wine & Garlic Sauce

SERVES 4–6

I usually spend summer holidays somewhere near the ocean. Nothing beats the smell of a huge pot of mussels steaming over an open fire, mixed with the cool ocean air.

Use a good-quality white wine, preferably the same one you are drinking. The wine forms a big part of the sauce, so don't use that bottle of dodgy wine you've had lying in the fridge for longer than you care to remember.

This recipe can easily be scaled up or down as needed.

EXTRA GEAR

Large colander
1 large cast-iron Dutch oven, with a lid
Heavy duty oven gloves or towels

INGREDIENTS

4 lb fresh black mussels
6 shallots
6 cloves garlic
1 large handful of fresh flat-leaf parsley
1 lemon
2 Tbsp olive oil
3 Tbsp butter
Salt
1 cup white wine (Sauvignon Blanc works well)
1 cup water
Cracked black pepper
1 loaf crusty bread

NOTES:
If you don't like wine, use beer. If you don't like beer, what's wrong with you?

PREP

1. Make sure the mussels are clean and good. Pop them in a colander and rinse under running water while you check them. They should be tightly closed. Tap any that are open lightly against the colander—if they don't close up within a minute, they are no good. Discard any that stay open or are heavily cracked.
2. If the mussels still have their beards attached, grip the beard between the paring knife and your thumb, and pull back to remove.
3. Thinly slice the shallots and mince the garlic.
4. Roughly chop the parsley. Cut the lemon in quarters, and again in half, so you have 8 wedges.

METHOD

5. Place the pot on medium-high heat and allow it to get up to temperature. Add the olive oil, and fry the shallots for 2 minutes until the edges start to color, stirring with a wooden spoon as you go.

6. Add the garlic, butter, and a good pinch of salt, and cook for another 2–3 minutes. Add the wine, and stir well, scraping the bottom of the pan as you go.

7. Add the water, and bring to the boil, then lower the heat to a strong simmer. Add the mussels, and pop the lid on the pot.

8. Cook covered for 3 minutes. Get the strongest guy around to give the pot a good shake (with the lid on) using the oven gloves or folded towels, then put it back on the heat. Cook for 2 minutes more, then open the pot.

9. Check the mussels. If many of them are still closed, put the lid back on, and cook for 2–3 minutes more, until the majority have opened up.

10. Squeeze the juice of a couple of lemon wedges over, season with salt and pepper, and add the parsley.

11. Gently stir through with the wooden spoon, lifting the bottom ones up as you go.

FINAL TOUCHES

12. Slice the bread. Serve in wide, shallow bowls along with bread slices. Let each guest tear off chunks of bread to mop the sauce up.

Gnocchi with Chorizo & Peas SERVES 2–4

Gnocchi is another Italian classic I just can't get enough of. Soft, pillowy nuggets of potato deliciousness, flash fried to a slight crisp. There is a good reason these little guys are loved the world over.

I won't lie though: making consistently great gnocchi is not easy, quick, or something you can master after two or three attempts. The amount of moisture and starch in the potatoes will always vary, as will the moisture absorption in the flour, so you are basically stuck with a bunch of variables you have no control over. The flour-to-potato ratio is key, as well as the way in which you handle the dough. Too little flour and the gnocchi will fall apart when you boil them. Too much flour and you will end up with potato-flavored rubber balls. While it is certainly essential to keep the dough as light and fluffy as possible, I for one actually like mine with a little more substance. Not hard and rubbery, but with a little more bite.

Most articles or recipes I've read go on a crusade about the supposed "correct" texture of gnocchi. It absolutely has to be soft and pillowy, almost melting in your mouth, like some sort of mystical potato fog. Truth be told, that kind of gnocchi you won't find around every street corner. Consistently making gnocchi to such a high standard is something reserved for Italian grandmothers (and even if they don't quite hit the mark every time, no one in their right mind would criticize an old Italian woman with a rolling pin in her hand).

The best advice I can give you is not to stress—just keep making them. Watch and feel the gnocchi as you make it, observe what you are doing and how the dough is feeling at every stage of the game, and compare results with previous batches. Next time, try adjusting the flour-to-potato ratio, and work on your technique.

Mastering gnocchi is not gonna happen quickly. You will, however, be able to make perfectly acceptable and delicious gnocchi sooner than you think, and that in itself is good enough for me.

EXTRA GEAR

Potato ricer
Sieve
Large work surface
Gnocchi board
Colander

INGREDIENTS

1 cup coarse / kosher salt for baking the potatoes
28 oz baking potatoes
9 oz flour, sifted, and extra for dusting (preferably cake flour)
1 egg
Water
1 tsp salt for boiling, and more for seasoning
1 Tbsp olive oil
3 oz chorizo
2 Tbsp butter
1 Tbsp sage, roughly chopped
1 cup peas
½ lemon, juiced and zested
Cracked black pepper

PREP

1. Pre-heat the oven to at 350°F / 180°C.

2. On a baking tray, pour out the salt for the potatoes and pat it out evenly. Add the potatoes on top. The salt helps to dry out the potatoes as they bake—and you want a drier potato mix to get the perfect consistency for your gnocchi.

3. Roast in the middle of the oven for about an hour or until the potatoes are soft all the way through.

4. Let the potatoes cool for about 15 minutes. Scoop out the flesh into a mixing bowl using a spoon, and discard the skins.

METHOD

5. Mash your potatoes with a potato ricer until smooth.

6. Add sifted flour to the potatoes, and gently knead. When the mix starts coming together well, add the egg, and mix again. This dough should be quite soft and pliable.

7. Tip your dough out onto a very large and lightly floured surface. Split the dough in half, and roll one half out into a sausage shape. Keep your hands, the dough, and the surface dry and lightly floured so nothing sticks together. There is a fine balance here, as you also don't want to knead this extra flour into the dough.

8. Once you have a long sausage shape, cut the gnocchi pieces using a sharp knife or dough cutter. The individual pieces should be about 1 inch / 2.5 cm in diameter.

9. Set them aside, and repeat with the other half. (If you have a gnocchi board, you can press each gnocco into its traditional shape by pressing it down with your thumb as you roll it over the lined surface.)

10. Bring a pot of salted water to a boil. Drop 10 gnocchi into the water at a time. The gnocchi are cooked after they rise to the surface and boil for another 20 seconds or so. Cook the gnocchi in batches, and scoop them out into a colander. Keep this water boiling to cook your peas.

11. Add the olive oil to a medium frying pan, and set on high heat. Slice the chorizo as thick you like it, and fry until just crispy. Remove from the pan, and keep warm in a bowl.

12. Add butter to the pan along with roughly chopped sage. When the butter is foaming, add a batch of gnocchi, but not enough to crowd the pan—each gnocco should be in contact with the pan. Panfry until lightly golden, and add to the same bowl as the chorizo.

13. While the second batch is frying, boil your peas. Once cooked, drain them.

14. Once all the gnocchi are fried, add them back to the pan as well as the chorizo and peas.

FINAL TOUCHES

15. Add the freshly squeezed lemon zest and juice, salt, and pepper, and serve immediately.

Prosciutto-Wrapped Baked Camembert

SERVES 2–4

This is one of my all-time favorite snacks to serve at dinner parties, cookouts, or really just about every opportunity I can. It's almost wrong to call it a recipe; it's *that* simple. It's way too delicious to not be in this book, though, so here you go.

Buy the best-quality ingredients you can find. Unlike stews, where you can take a tough cut of meat and cook it low and slow to perfection, quick and simple "slap together" recipes like this offer no such chances at redemption. What you put in is what you get out.

Get the best-quality bread, prosciutto, camembert, and basil pesto you can find, then give them a chance to shine. You'll understand what I mean when you take your first bite.

EXTRA GEAR

Egg lifter

INGREDIENTS

Few sprigs thyme
1 loaf ciabatta or baguette
1 wheel camembert
1 tsp basil pesto
Pinch chili flakes
Couple thin slices prosciutto
Olive oil

NOTES:
This recipe also works really well in a smoker if you have one. Just lay the prepared cheese on aluminum foil, and smoke until the cheese goes gooey.

You can replace the camembert with brie if you want; it works just as well.

PREP

1. Preheat the oven to 350°F / 180°C.
2. Strip the thyme leaves from the sprigs.

METHOD

3. Slice the bread, and lay the slices on a baking sheet.
4. Carefully slice the camembert right through the middle (so you have two wheels), and lay them on a cutting board, rind side down.

5. Spread the pesto on one half, and sprinkle with chili flakes. Close the camembert back up like a sandwich, with the pesto and chili flakes in the middle. Wrap the camembert with prosciutto strips, leaving the ends underneath the cheese so the cheese's weight keeps them in place.

6. Put the cheese on the baking sheet, with the bread arranged around it. Drizzle olive oil over everything, and sprinkle with thyme leaves.

7. Bake in the oven for about 10–15 minutes until the cheese goes gooey and starts to run out the side. Turn the bread over after 10 minutes or so. Remove the cheese from oven as soon as it starts to ooze out (lifting it with an egg lifter), and set aside to cool.

8. Keep toasting the bread until they are browned to your liking.

FINAL TOUCHES

9. Serve on a wood board with a sharp knife. People can slice off sections and scoop it up with the bread. Have some napkins around—this one can get messy.

Crème Brûlée SERVES 6

Crème brûlée, translated as *burnt cream*, is one of those fancy French desserts that I used to think could only be made by French dudes with large moustaches in chef's whites and big floppy hats. Not so! Once you get the hang of it, it's actually pretty straightforward—and a guaranteed hit.

Soft, sweet, velvety smooth custard that is cool on your tongue, together with a somewhat bitter, somewhat sweet crunchy topping that is still slightly warm. It just does not get any better than this.

In terms of ingredients, it's a very simple recipe. The trick is in the technique. But don't worry—it's really easy. Follow the recipe step by step, and you can't go wrong!

A side note: once you've made this for someone, they are bound to ask for it again and again and again, so choose your guests wisely.

EXTRA GEAR

Dishcloth
Kettle
Slotted spoon
Oven tray with high walls that can hold 6 ramekins
6 ramekins
Jam jar lifter
Blowtorch

INGREDIENTS

1 vanilla bean
2 cups whipping cream
6 eggs
½ cup granulated sugar + roughly 2 tsp more for serving

NOTES:

We won't be using the egg whites in this recipe. You can make meringues or mousses with the leftover egg white, or freeze it for later use.

To learn how to work with real vanilla beans, see page 12.

PREP

1. Preheat the oven to 300°F /150°C.

2. Split the vanilla bean in half lengthways with a paring knife, and scrape out the seeds with the back of the knife. Keep the husk.

METHOD

3. First, we need to make an egg custard mixture. Pour the cream into a small saucepan, and put the pan on medium heat. Add the vanilla seeds as well as the empty husk into the cream.

4. Heat the cream to just before boiling point, keeping an eye on it and stirring occasionally.

5. Separate the egg whites from the yolks (see page 37; you won't need the egg whites for this recipe), and add ½ cup of sugar to the yolks. Wet the dishcloth under the tap, and wring it out. Roll it up lengthwise, and form a circle on your work surface. Place the bowl with egg yolks on top of this circle. The wet cloth will grip the bowl as well as the work surface, making it possible for you to whisk the eggs without using your other hand to hold the bowl—you'll need this later. Whisk the eggs and sugar together until they go slightly pale; no need to get too crazy here.

6. By now, the cream should have come up to temperature, and the smell of vanilla should be filling your kitchen. Take a deep whiff—gorgeous, isn't it? Remove the saucepan from heat, and fish out and discard the vanilla husk with a fork.

7. Put on a full kettle of water—you will need it shortly. Now, we need to get the eggs and cream mixed together. This is the stage where things can go horribly wrong. If we add the hot cream to the cold eggs, the eggs will start to cook and form scrambled eggs, which is definitely not what we want. This is where technique comes in. We need to temper the eggs or, in other words, get the eggs up to the temperature of the cream gradually to avoid it changing its texture (i.e., turn into scrambled eggs). To do this, hold the whisk in your dominant hand and the saucepan of hot cream in the other. Start by pouring a dash of cream into the eggs, whisking as you go. Once the cream is incorporated into the eggs, add a dash more, and keep whisking. Keep going like that (you can increase the size of the "dash" every time), until you have added half the cream.

8. At this stage, the eggs will be tempered, so add the last half of the cream in two large batches, whisking as you go. Once it is all combined, you will notice foam forming on top of the mixture. This is the egg white that wasn't separated from the yolk (try doing a better job separating the eggs next time to save some hassle at this point). Not to worry. Let the mixture settle so all the foam comes to the top, then scoop it off with a slotted spoon, letting the liquid drip back into the bowl. Discard the foam. You now have an uncooked egg custard mixture.

9. Next we need to make a water bath or bain-marie. Take the damp dishcloth, flatten it out, and place it at the bottom of a high-walled oven tray. This is to stop the ramekins from moving about once we add water to the tray. Place the ramekins on top of the dishcloth, then divide the custard mixture between them. Gently pour the hot water into the oven tray until it reaches about halfway up the side of the ramekins. Take care not to get any water inside the ramekins.

10. Carefully transfer the oven tray to the oven, and bake for 50 minutes at 300°F / 150°C. Once done, carefully remove the tray from the oven, and get the ramekins out of the hot water ASAP. Let the ramekins cool down to room temperature, then pop them in the fridge for at least 4–6 hours—overnight is even better.

FINAL TOUCHES

11. To serve, take the ramekins out of the fridge, and pour in some sugar so it coats the top. Swirl the sugar around so it sticks to the surface of the custard. Pour out any extra sugar that does not stick into the next ramekin, and repeat the process. Add a little more sugar as you go until all 6 ramekins have a light, even coating of sugar on top. You don't want too thick a sugar layer on top or it will be too hard to crack through with a spoon.

12. Finally, get the blow torch out (oh yeah!) and gently caramelize the sugar on top of the custards. Keep moving the flame around so you don't burn one spot while the others still require work. When all the sugar has liquidized, caramelize it further by holding the flame still for a few seconds. The sugar will start to burn and form a deep, dark caramel. You want a deep dark color at least in some spots, but don't overdo it. The bitterness of the dark caramel works beautifully with the sweet, smooth creaminess of the custard. The dish is literally called *burnt cream*, after all.

13. And there you have it, you've just made crème brûlée. Hand these bad boys over to your lucky guests, and enjoy!

Badass Baking

Cheese & Onion Beer Bread SERVES 4–6

If you absolutely suck at baking bread, this is the recipe for you. There is no kneading, no proofing, no shaping—just mix all the ingredients together and bake. It's as simple as it gets.

Basically, if you mess this one up, you should hang up your apron and consider taking up another hobby . . . maybe stamp collecting.

Jokes aside, this bread is easy and delicious and requires minimal ingredients, skills, or equipment. Also, it contains beer.

EXTRA GEAR

9″ x 5″ loaf pan
Oven gloves / dish towels

INGREDIENTS

4 Tbsp butter, plus extra to grease
½ cup diced onion (plus a few thin slices to garnish)
1 cup grated cheddar cheese (plus more to garnish)
3 cups self-rising flour
1 12-oz bottle of beer
1 Tbsp white sugar
1 tsp salt

NOTES:
You can leave out the onions and cheese if you just want classic beer bread.

PREP

1. Preheat the oven to 375°F / 190°C.
2. Lightly grease the inside of the loaf tin with butter, melt the rest of it, and divide the melted butter into two containers.
3. Finely chop the onion, and grate the cheese.

METHOD

4. Add all the ingredients to a mixing bowl, leaving half the butter aside. Mix with a wooden spoon until fairly smooth, except for the odd small lump here and there.
5. Spoon the batter into the loaf pan, and flatten out the top with the spoon. Sprinkle a few slices of onion and a little more grated cheese on top.
6. Drizzle the remaining butter over the top, then pop the pan in the oven and bake for 50–55 minutes until golden brown.
7. Stick a toothpick inside the bread to check for doneness. The toothpick should come out fairly clean, except for the odd crumb. If the toothpick comes out with wet bits of dough stuck to it, bake for another 5–10 minutes, and check again.
8. Allow to cool for 30 minutes before slicing, if you can wait.

FINAL TOUCHES

9. Serve with slabs of butter and more cheese. Drink some beer while you're at it. You deserve it!

Double-Boozy Chocolate & Cherry Cake

SERVES 8

Look, I'll be honest. I haven't baked a cake in my life. Not even this one. My deadline was approaching, and I couldn't afford this one to flop. I enlisted the help of my incredibly beautiful, talented, and amazing girlfriend, Claire, to make this one become a reality.

Sure, I was there on the sidelines. I gave flavoring and styling ideas and asked all sorts amateurish questions while Claire calmly put this masterpiece together. I did totally help with the decorating (yeah, okay, she had to . . . um . . . correct a few things). Claire assures me that this cake is foolproof, though, and I believe whatever she says (it's safer that way). In my professional cake-judging opinion, I can conclude that it's pretty damn awesome.

The cake itself is drenched in a coffee-and-rum syrup. The filling is a layer of thick, luxurious chocolate ganache frosting (see sidebar), topped with a layer of light vanilla cream filling and a cherry and red wine compote (see sidebar). As if that were not enough deliciousness going on already, we smother it all with another chocolate ganache, this time in the form of a glaze.

To kick things up a final notch on the fancy scale, we made chocolate shards (Claire did, but I totally helped by holding the baking sheet or something).

NOTES:

Ganache is a glaze, sauce, or frosting filling used extensively in cakes, tarts, and pastries. The name might sound scary, but don't worry—it is essentially just chocolate and cream in specific ratios. We use two different ones in this recipe: a frosting and a glaze.

The cherry compote is made by slow-cooking cherries in red wine, sugar, and some spices. Like most things with fancy French names, it's way easier to make than you'd imagine, and also way more delicious. Those French dudes with the floppy white hats know a thing or two about cooking, you gotta hand them that.

A good rule to follow when using wine in your cooking is to cook with wine you would drink. Don't use the cheap stuff!

To learn how to work with real vanilla beans, see page 12.

EXTRA GEAR

2 springform cake tins
Electric beater
Baking paper
Sieve
Cake skewer (or wooden kebab stick)

INGREDIENTS

Red wine cherry compote

1 vanilla bean (or 3 tsp vanilla extract)
¾ cup light brown sugar
1 cinnamon stick
5 whole star anise
2 cups red wine
2 cups cherries (frozen, fresh, or canned)

Sponge cake

2 cups butter, softened at room temp for an hour
2 cups castor sugar
¼ tsp salt
1 tsp vanilla extract
2 cups eggs
1¾ cups cake flour
½ cup cocoa powder, plus extra to garnish

Rum soaking syrup

2 vanilla beans (or 6 tsp vanilla extract)
2 sticks cinnamon
1 cup brown sugar
3 cups water
¾ cup rum
1 orange, juiced and zested

Whipped vanilla cream

2 cups thick cream
2 Tbsp icing sugar, sifted
Vanilla seeds, reserved from 1 vanilla bean (or 3 tsp vanilla extract)

Chocolate ganache frosting

9 oz dark chocolate (70 percent)
1 cup cream

Chocolate glaze

7 oz dark chocolate (70 percent)
1 cup cream

PREP

Red wine cherry compote:

1. Cut the vanilla bean in half. Scrape to remove the seeds (see page 12), and set aside. Reserve these seeds to make the whipped cream later.

2. In a wide, flat pot, add the scraped vanilla bean, sugar, cinnamon, and star anise. Watch as the sugar begins to bubble and turn brown, mostly unevenly and very quickly. Just swirl the pan around gently, until it is evenly caramelized, but don't stir it with a spoon. Add the red wine and stand back as it bubbles, spits, and steams. Continue to cook the wine until the caramel has dissolved, then add your cherries, and cook for another 2 minutes.

3. Set aside to cool, then chill in the fridge.

Sponge cake:

4. Preheat the oven to 340°F / 170°C.

5. Grease two 10-inch (25 cm) springform cake baking tins.

6. In a large mixing bowl, add the butter and sugar. Beat with an electric mixer until it is well creamed and lighter in color.

7. Add the salt, vanilla, and eggs one at a time, mixing continuously as you go. It may appear to not be mixing, but when you add the flour in later, it will be perfect, I promise.

8. Sift the flour and cocoa powder into the egg-and-butter mix, and fold it in using a rubber spatula or wooden spoon. Once you see an evenly brown mix, stop mixing! An overbeaten or overly mixed cake batter will be dense, and you'll see tunnels in your cake dough when you slice it.

9. Divide the mix evenly between the two cake tins and smooth out the top gently. Bake at 340°F / 170°C, taking care not to open the oven until at least 40 minutes into baking. Keep your oven's temperature at that heat; if you jump beyond that, it may cause a peak in the middle and a burnt top crust. Open the oven door slightly, and, using a skewer, pierce your cake in the middle. The skewer should come out clean when the cake is done. Remove from the oven, and cool on racks.

Chocolate paper garnish:

10. Using a double boiler, gently melt your chocolate, and spread it out evenly onto baking paper on a baking tray. Spread the chocolate in as thin and even a

layer as you can, making sure there are no spots where you can see the baking paper through the chocolate. Allow it to set at room temperature, then chill for 15 minutes before serving.

METHOD

Rum soaking syrup:

11. Split the vanilla beans in half lengthways with a paring knife, and scrape out the seeds with the back of the knife.

12. Add the seeds as well as the husks to a small saucepan. Add the rest of the ingredients for the rum soaking syrup, and cook for around 3 minutes until syrupy.

13. Remove one of the sponges from the cake tin. The cakes will not be 100 percent flat. To ensure an even layering, you will need to make one of the sponges flatter by trimming the peak. Using a long serrated bread knife, carefully slice off the peak using small strokes, and return the sponge to the baking tin.

14. Using a pastry brush, liberally soak both sponges with the syrup. Let them sit for 10 minutes, then flip them over, and use the rest of the syrup to soak the cakes.

Whipped vanilla cream:

15. Whisk all the ingredients together and chill in the fridge.

Chocolate ganache frosting:

16. Chop your chocolate. Heat the cream in a small sauce pan; it does not need to boil. Add the chopped chocolate, and whisk in gently until glossy and even.

17. Cool for around 15 minutes, then whisk vigorously for a few minutes to cool and thicken it. You can also use an electric beater and whip it until it becomes a firm frosting.

Chocolate glaze:

18. Chop your chocolate. Heat the cream in a small saucepan; it does not need to boil. Add the chopped chocolate, and whisk it in gently until glossy and even.

19. Cool for around 10 minutes, and then get ready to use it right away.

FINAL TOUCHES

20. Transfer the evenly cut sponge to your serving plate. Soak the sponge with half of the syrup from the red wine cherry compote. Spread half of the ganache frosting onto the sponge, then half of the whipped cream and half of the cherries.

21. Top with the other sponge. Spread the remainder of the ganache frosting onto the cake, then pour the chocolate glaze over the top. Add the rest of the cherries to the whipped cream, and dollop liberally on top.

22. Break the chocolate paper into rough shards, and pierce the top of the cake as you like. Dust with cocoa powder.

Pumpkin Tart SERVES 6–8

As a South African, writing a recipe for pumpkin pie for an American audience would be like might seem a little like an Eskimo writing a guide to survival in the Sahara desert.

Instead, I give you my recipe for pumpkin tart (or *Pampoentert*, as we call it), the second cousin (twice removed) of the classic American pumpkin pie.

EXTRA GEAR

Food processor
Roasting tray
Sieve

INGREDIENTS

Roasted pumpkin puree

2 lb pumpkin
2 Tbsp neutral oil
2 Tbsp white sugar
1 Tbsp butter
1 tsp cinnamon
Salt

Pumpkin tart

1½ Tbsp flour
1 cup cream
2 tsp salt
¼ cup white sugar
¼ cup dark brown sugar
2 oz melted butter, plus extra to grease the dish
3 eggs
3 cups roasted pumpkin puree
¼ cup pumpkin seeds

PREP

1. Preheat the oven to 350°F / 180°C.

2. Cut the pumpkin into cubes.

3. Add all the ingredients for roasted pumpkin puree to the roasting tray, and mix well with your hands to coat the cubed pumpkin. Roast for 25–35 minutes until soft and crispy-edged.

4. Let the pumpkin cool to room temperature. Blitz in a food processor until smooth. Pop the puree in a mixing bowl.

METHOD

Pumpkin Tart:

5. Sift the flour with a sieve.

6. Add the sifted flour, cream, salt, both sugars, and melted butter to the mixing bowl with the pumpkin puree, and whisk until smooth.

7. Carefully and one by one, crack an egg into the mixture, and whisk in.

8. Butter the baking dish, pour in the pumpkin mixture, and bake for 20–30 minutes. The center should look slightly soft and barely cooked. If you tap the side of the dish, it should wobble a bit but not cause large ripples.

FINAL TOUCHES

9. Toast pumpkin seeds in a pan with 1 Tbsp of oil and a generous pinch of salt. Sprinkle on top, and serve.

PLAAS HIERDIE KANT
OP BAKPLAAT

Cinnamon Rolls SERVES 6–8

These cinnamon rolls are a must-have in the culinary arsenal of any man who suffers from the dreaded ADAC (Avoid Dishwashing at All Costs).

You know those large dinner parties that turn into somewhat civilized booze fests and usually leave you with a pile of dishes and a number of (worse-for-wear-looking) friends dozing on couches and spare beds in the morning? These little cinnamon rolls will sort that right out.

Simply bake a batch of these in the morning. The smell will drift through the house, and before you know it, you will have a face peeking into the kitchen asking, "Whatcha doing?" You reply with, "Oh, nothing much. I got up early to bake you guys some cinnamon rolls. Want some coffee?"

If you have semidecent friends (that part is essential to the plan; if you mainly have friends in low places, abandon ship), this should trigger some feelings of guilt. They've trashed your place, and you're still so nice to make them delicious things in the morning.

With any luck, you should hear a somewhat reluctant "Anything I could do to help?" Now you're golden. Simply reply with a friendly, "Nah, it's cool, I got this, but you can start cleaning up in the kitchen if you want."

Hopefully by now, more faces will have started appearing, making all of them too embarrassed to decline. After some low grumbling and a few broken glasses, you should find yourself with a sparkly clean kitchen in no time, crisis averted.

EXTRA GEAR

Baking paper
Sieve
Large work surface
Pastry brush

INGREDIENTS

Cinnamon rolls

2½ Tbsp cinnamon
¼ cup + 2 Tbsp sugar
1 cup milk
¾ cup + 4 Tbsp + 1 Tbsp butter
2¼ tsp instant yeast
½ tsp salt
4 cups all-purpose flour, plus extra for dusting
Oil, to grease the bowl

Glaze

8 Tbsp powdered sugar
3 Tbsp lemon juice

PREP

1. Heat the oven to 350°F / 180°C.
2. Line a baking dish with baking paper.
3. Mix 1½ Tbsp cinnamon with 2 Tbsp sugar, and set aside.

METHOD

4. Melt the milk and butter together in a saucepan, but do not boil or overheat. It should be warm enough for you to dip your finger in comfortably. Add the yeast and 1 tbsp sugar, and whisk it up. Leave to activate for 10 minutes.
5. In a large mixing bowl, sift the flour with a sieve. Add 1 tbsp cinnamon and the salt together. Add the milk and yeast mixture, and stir up into a sticky dough.
6. Tip out the mix onto a floured surface, and knead lightly into a ball for about 5 minutes.

7. Oil the mixing bowl lightly, and put the dough back into the bowl, covering it with a damp cloth. Leave in a warm place to rise for an hour or until it has doubled in size.

8. On a lightly floured surface, roll out your dough into a rectangle. The dough should be ¼-inch thick. The long side should be facing you. Melt 4 Tbsp butter, and use it to brush the dough, reserving about 1 Tbsp for the top. Sprinkle evenly with the cinnamon and sugar mix you had prepared earlier, reserving about 1 Tbsp for the top.

9. Roll the dough tightly starting from one end—this is a fun two-man job. Once it is tightly rolled, you will have a long sausage. Cut the rolls using a sharp knife or dough cutter. Each roll should be about 2 inches / 5 cm long.

10. Place them evenly on a baking sheet. Brush the tops of the rolls with the remaining 1 Tbsp of butter, and sprinkle the remaining 1 Tbsp of cinnamon sugar on top. Leave to rise in a warm place for about 15 minutes.

11. Bake on the middle shelf in the oven for around 20–25 minutes or until the rolls are golden brown.

FINAL TOUCHES

12. Melt the remaining 1 Tbsp of butter, and brush the rolls as they come out the oven. Next, mix the powdered sugar and lemon juice together, and drizzle over the rolls to glaze.

Pecan & Walnut Pie with Vanilla Ice Cream SERVES 6–8

Pecan pie is as American as they come, so you should really know how to slap one together yourself. I used a mix of pecans and walnuts in this version, but you can certainly go full pecan if you want.

While it's certainly delicious to eat cold, I prefer eating it warmed up with a blob of good quality vanilla ice cream. Buy some ice cream if you are of the slightly less industrious persuasion, or make your own at home (see ice cream recipe on page 149). It's easier than you think, and totally worth the effort.

EXTRA GEAR

10-inch (25 cm) pie dish
Baking paper
Rolling pin

INGREDIENTS

Pastry

1 egg
9 Tbsp (4½ oz) butter, chilled and chopped (plus extra to grease)
1¼ cup cake flour (plus extra to dust)
¼ tsp salt
4 Tbsp castor sugar
2–3 Tbsp ice water

Filling

1 cup golden or maple syrup
1 cup dark brown sugar
2 tsp vanilla extract
4 Tbsp butter
11 oz pecans
4 oz walnuts
4 eggs
2 Tbsp milk
Salt

PREP

1. Preheat the oven to 400°F / 200°C.

Pastry

2. For the pastry, separate the egg yolk from the white (see page 37). You won't be using the egg white for this recipe.

3. Butter a 10-inch (25 cm) pie dish.

4. Add the butter and flour together in a mixing bowl. Add the salt, and rub together gently with your fingers until it resembles breadcrumbs. Add the sugar and egg yolk, and mix with a spoon.

5. Add the ice water in a tablespoon at a time. (You may only need to use 1 Tbsp of the water, depending on the size of your egg and the humidity of your flour, butter, and sugar.) Keep mixing until it starts to come together as a sticky ball. You want to be able to knead it into a ball, but it should not stick to your hand.

6. Form the dough into a flat disc, then fold a sheet of baking paper over it, and chill in the fridge for at least 15 minutes.

METHOD

7. On a lightly floured surface, roll out the pastry with a rolling pin until 2 mm thick. Gently roll the pastry up over the rolling pin and transfer to the pie dish. Pat the pastry into the dish evenly, lifting as you need to ensure there are no air bubbles. Press the pastry flat against the sides and the rim. There will be excess, uneven edges—that's fine; you will trim them off when the pie is cooked. Chill the pastry in the fridge for 10 minutes.

Filling

8. In a small saucepan, add the syrup, sugar, and vanilla, and melt together gently on a medium heat. Turn up the heat, and cook on high for 3 minutes, stirring regularly. Add the butter, a pinch of salt, and stir in. Set aside to cool.

9. Chop the nuts. In a mixing bowl, whisk together the eggs and milk, then slowly add the cooled syrup mix, and whisk well. Layer the chopped nuts evenly over the pastry in the pie dish, then carefully pour in the syrup filling.

10. Bake at 400°F / 200°C for 10 minutes, then turn down to 320°F / 160°C, and bake for another 20 minutes. Rotate your pie in the oven to ensure even baking, and bake for another 20 minutes or until it becomes firm in the middle.

11. Allow to cool slightly. Using a small and sharp paring knife, gently shave the rim of the excess pastry off. I like to eat these bits, but you can also leave it as is if you like the rustic look.

FINAL TOUCHES

12. Serve with ice cream or just as it is, warm or chilled.

Blueberry Muffins SERVES 6

Everyone should bake at least one tray of great muffins in their life. No, the herb-infused variety you baked in college (fun as they no doubt were) does not count.

I love having fresh muffins with coffee for breakfast, but having to go outside to a bakery to buy them clashes with my "No Pants Before Coffee" rule in the mornings.

In the interest of public safety, have a go at baking these this weekend; you may just avoid some serious mental scarring in your neighborhood.

EXTRA GEAR

Muffin pan,12 small cups or 6 large cups

INGREDIENTS

4 oz butter, plus extra to grease
1 cup dark brown sugar
1 tsp vanilla extract
½ cup orange juice
Zest of 2 oranges
2 cups cake flour
1 tsp baking soda
½ tsp salt
½ tsp cinnamon
½ tsp nutmeg
½ tsp dried ginger
2 eggs
1½ cups blueberries

NOTES:
This recipe makes either 12 normal-sized muffins or 6 large ones, depending on the muffin pan you use. I like to use a large 6-cup muffin pan.

PREP

1. Preheat the oven to 350°F / 180°C.
2. Grease the muffin tin or put cupcake papers in the cups.
3. In a small saucepan on medium heat, combine the butter, sugar, vanilla, orange juice, and zest. Heat until a sauce is formed, taking care to remove from the heat as soon as it is melted together—you don't want to cook this mixture. Set aside to cool.

METHOD

4. In a mixing bowl, sift the dry ingredients together, and mix well.
5. Crack the eggs one at a time into a small bowl, then add to the warm butter mixture, whisking well to incorporate. Add this mix to the dry ingredients. Mix well with a spatula, but do not overmix.
6. Add the blueberries.
7. Spoon the mix into the tin, filling them up ¾ of the way.
8. Bake for 20–25 minutes in the middle of the oven. To test their doneness, insert a cake skewer or a toothpick—it should come out clean.

FINAL TOUCHES

9. Serve immediately with jam and cream or just thick slabs of butter.

Upside Down Ginger & Pear Cake SERVES 8

This cake is one of my favorite recipes in this book, hands down. Coming from a man with unnaturally high levels of fruit aversion, that's saying something.

I was allergic to many types of fruit as kid, so I grew up not eating any fruit at all. I've outgrown the allergies long ago (except pineapple, it's still the devil), but somehow I just don't like the taste and texture of fresh fruit. But poach or bake them, when the taste and texture changes considerably, and I'll eat them, no problem.

Cooking the pears in caramel transforms them even further, from those weird-looking things on trees I despised as a kid to amber-colored jewels of deliciousness, almost good enough to make me consider eating fresh pears.

Pop those beauties on top of cake, and you have yourself one of the best cakes I've ever tasted.

EXTRA GEAR

10-inch (25 cm) spring-form cake tin
Baking paper
Electric beater or stand mixer
Sieve
Cake skewer (or wooden kebab stick)

INGREDIENTS

Pears

- 7 Tbsp (3½ oz) butter, plus extra to grease
- 3 medium pears
- 1½ cups brown sugar, packed

Batter

- 18 Tbsp (9 oz) butter, room temperature
- 1 cup brown sugar, packed
- 4 eggs
- 1½ cups self-rising flour
- ¼ of salt
- 1 tsp cinnamon
- 2 Tbsp milk
- 1 tsp vanilla extract

PREP

1. Preheat the oven to 350°F / 180°C.

2. Grease a 10-inch nonstick cake dish like a springform tin or deep dish pie tin. Using a springform tin makes the cake easier to remove.

3. Cut a circle of baking paper big enough to cover the base of the dish, and pop it in to the bottom, making sure it is nicely tucked into the sides.

METHOD

Pears:

4. Peel the pears, remove the seeds, and cut into eighths.

5. In a nonstick pan, heat the butter and sugar. They should bubble together and form a light caramel. You don't need the caramel to be even and shiny; it just needs to come together nicely. Take care not to stir or mix too much, as it will crystallize and turn to fudge bits instead of a smooth sauce.

6. Add the pears to this bubbly caramel, and cook them until brown on both sides. Set aside.

Batter:

7. In a large mixing bowl, cream the butter and sugar together with a hand mixer (or use a countertop stand mixer) until they are well whipped and pale.

8. Crack the eggs one by one into the mixture, whisking well to ensure each one is well incorporated.

9. It should look like it has curdled a bit, but this will change once you add the rest of the ingredients.

10. Next, sift the flour into the mix along with the salt and cinnamon. Hand-mix to incorporate. Once it has come together, add the milk and vanilla extract to loosen the batter to a more pourable consistency.

11. Arrange the pears in the bottom of the tin in a spiral pattern, taking care to tuck them in nicely together. Pour the remaining caramel over them.

12. Spoon in the batter, and spread evenly with a spoon, pushing it out to ensure no air pockets are left in the batter.

13. Bake in the middle of the oven for 30–35 minutes. Only open the oven after 30 minutes—not before—to test, or the cake might droop in the middle. Insert a cake skewer in the middle—it should come out clean when done.

14. Remove from the oven, and cool for about 10 minutes. Slide a knife carefully around the edges to loosen. Then, place a large-lipped plate over the top of the cake tin, and carefully, but without hesitation, flip it over. If you are lucky, you will feel the cake gently drop out. If not, carefully unlatch the springform to loosen the cake. Remove the bottom and the baking paper.

FINAL TOUCHES

15. Serve with lashings of whipped cream or chilled custard.

My Food Heritage

Ta' Ellatjie se Melktert (Aunt Ella's Milk Tart)

SERVES 6–8

One of my earliest food memories is eating melkpap (milk porridge), which our nanny, Marie, made early in the mornings. This milk porridge was the filling used in the melktert (milk tart) she was baking, and I always got the task of clearing out every morsel left over in the pot with a wooden spoon.

As you can see in the picture below, I took this task rather seriously. If I happened to be in the bath when Marie bellowed out that my services were required, trivial matters like drying off and clothes suddenly took a large dip in the order of priorities.

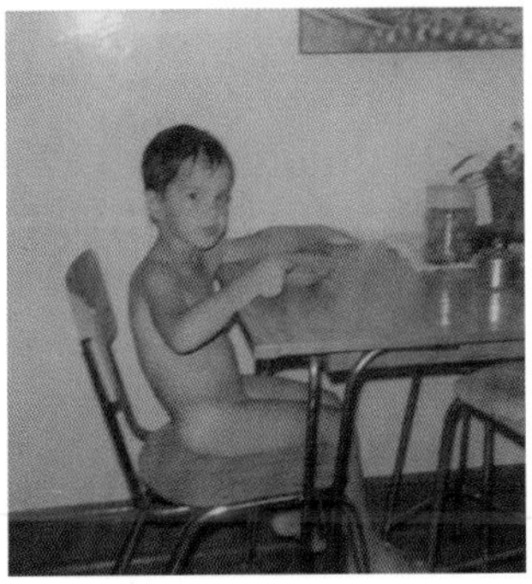

When I grew up in Heidelberg, Ta' Ellatjie (Aunt Ella) was known far and wide as the Melktert Queen, and everyone lined up to buy them. I really wanted to include her recipe in this book, so I phoned my dad, who managed to track her down. She graciously offered to give me her famous recipe. And when my dad arrived to fetch the recipe around lunchtime, she had already whipped up two variations of melktert earlier that morning so he could choose the one he liked best.

I'm pretty sure Ta' Ellatjie can whip up a melktert in her sleep with one hand tied behind her back, so there is no reason you can't do it, either, but I suggest you keep your eyes open and use both hands, just to be safe.

EXTRA GEAR

Rolling pin
10-inch (25 cm) tart tin / dish

INGREDIENTS

1 sheet ready-made puff pastry
½ cup cake flour, plus extra for dusting
Butter, for greasing
3½ cups milk
1 stick cinnamon
½ cup white sugar
½ tsp salt
2 tsp cornstarch
3 eggs
1 tsp vanilla extract

PREP

1. Preheat oven to 400°F / 200°C.

2. Lay out the puff pastry on a floured work surface, and roll it out with a rolling pin until it is wide enough to cover the tart tin. It should be about ¼-inch thick. Grease the inside of the tart tin with butter. Lay the pastry out in the tin, and trim off the edges sticking over the outer edge of the rim. Place the tin in the fridge to stay cool while you make the filling.

3. Add 3 cups of milk and a cinnamon stick to a pot. Heat until just below boiling. Remove from heat and set aside.

METHOD

4. In the mixing bowl, add flour, sugar, salt, and cornstarch together, along with ½ cup of milk, and mix into a smooth paste.

5. Remove the cinnamon stick from the warm milk, and add the flour paste to the pot. Return this mixture to the heat, and bring to the boil while stirring. Reduce heat, and simmer for a minute or two until the mixture thickens up.

6. Remove from heat and add the eggs one at a time, stirring to combine properly before adding the next egg. Add the vanilla extract, and mix well.

7. Remove the tart tin from the fridge, and pour in the filling. Bake for 35 minutes in the middle of the oven. The tart will rise up about an inch or so as it bakes, but fear not, everything is okay.

8. When the top starts to form a slight dome in the middle and has browned nicely, remove the tart from the oven. Allow to cool to lukewarm temperature.

FINAL TOUCHES

9. Many South Africans like to sprinkle cinnamon over the top at this stage, but I prefer my melktert without. Serve cold or slightly warmed with afternoon tea, or, if you are like me, have melktert for breakfast. Just do us all a favor and keep your clothes on.

Souskluitjies SERVES 6

When it comes to childhood favorites, *souskluitjies* (an Afrikaans word pronounced "sows-clay-keys" and directly translated as *sauce dumplings*) sits squarely at the top of my list. These cinnamon-flavored dumplings cooked in scandalous amounts of butter and sugar is wintertime comfort food at its finest. This traditional dish is a favorite across South Africa, particularly within Afrikaans families (like mine). There are many different ways of making these, and of course everyone will claim that their way is the best—and the right way to do it. In truth, your preference will most likely be for the version you first encountered as a child, most likely made by your ouma (grandmother).

My favorite version is the one below, lovingly made for me (countless, countless times) by Anita Swart, a close family friend. Our families had get-togethers at least once a week, and I requested this treasured dish at every opportunity that I could. The problem was that everyone else was not as keen as I was to eat souskluitjies every single Sunday, so the majority rule from the Dessert Committee often got me outvoted. Noticing my disappointment at the lack of souskluitjies in my life, Tannie Anita (Aunt Anita) often made a batch specially for me to take home. I would return home overjoyed, carefully balancing the dish in the car to avoid the sauce spilling out as if my life depended on it. I would plan exactly how I was going to ration myself on this big batch of *kluitjies* (as it's affectionately nicknamed), so I could spread the deliciousness over as many days as possible. In truth, that never really panned out anyway—I scoffed it down as fast as I could. Once we got home, wouldn't you know it, suddenly everyone was in the mood for kluitjies, too, and I had to (at times, rather reluctantly) share my bounty.

Tannie Anita could never really give me the recipe, as she cooks kluitjies by feel, "a little bit of this, a little bit of that" kind of style. I phoned her up the other day and explained that I would really love to include this childhood treasure in my book, but I needed a concrete recipe. She generously cooked up a batch the next day, measuring the ingredients and writing them down for me.

I haven't been this excited about cooking something in a *long* time. I have tried a number of different recipes I've found in books and on the Internet, but none of them has the taste and texture just right. When I prepared this recipe, it was like a revelation. Everything smelled right, looked right, and just felt right. After I shot the image for this recipe, it was time for a taste. As I took my first bite, I was transported back to being that nine-year-old boy, balancing the dish in the back of the car. I was smiling from ear to ear. It's really amazing how nostalgia and food intertwines to bring you a level of comfort and happiness that money simply cannot buy.

INGREDIENTS

1 cup all-purpose flour
½ tsp salt
4 cups full-cream milk
4 Tbsp ground cinnamon
1 cup sugar
1 cinnamon stick
Butter, loads of it (just under ½ lb)
2 tsp vanilla extract

PREP

1. Add the flour and salt to a mixing bowl, and whisk into a smooth paste using about ¾ cup of the milk.

2. Mix the ground cinnamon with the sugar.

3. Add remaining milk to a pot along with the cinnamon stick, and heat to just below boiling.

4. Cut the butter into small cubes, and set aside.

METHOD

5. Add the flour paste to the hot milk, and keep whisking until it reaches boiling point.

6. Reduce heat, and simmer for about 5 minutes until the mixture is thick, constantly whisking as you go. Remove from heat, and whisk in 1 Tbsp butter and the vanilla extract. Set aside.

7. In a baking dish, lay down a thick layer of the cinnamon-sugar mix you prepared and lots of butter cubes. Spoon dollops of the cooked mixture on top using a tablespoon, leaving some space between them. Lay down another layer of cinnamon sugar and butter, and repeat until no more mixture is left.

8. Set aside to cool.

FINAL TOUCHES

9. To serve, bake for 15–20 minutes (and no longer) in a preheated oven at 350°F / 180°C.

10. Remove from the oven, and serve piping hot with some vanilla ice cream.

NOTES:
If the mixture gets too lumpy, use an electric beater to smooth things out again.

Mom's Apple Pudding

SERVES 6–8

This pudding will always remind me of my mother, who sadly passed away during the writing of this book.

Normally, I'd advocate using fresh apples and cooking them down yourself, as well as making your own caramel rather than using imitation essence. However, this is Mom's apple pudding, and I shall not dare alter it.

EXTRA GEAR

12″ x 8″ rectangular baking dish
Small saucepan

INGREDIENTS

Pudding

1 can apple slices (16 oz)
2 Tbsp butter (plus extra for greasing)
1 cup sugar
3 eggs
¼ cup milk
1 cup cake flour
1 tsp baking powder
½ tsp salt

Sauce

4 Tbsp butter
½ cup sugar
½ cup milk
1 tsp caramel essence

PREP

1. Preheat the oven to 350°F / 180°C.
2. Open the can of apples, and drain off the liquid.
3. Grease the inside of the baking dish with butter.

METHOD

Pudding:

4. Cream the butter and sugar in a mixing bowl. Incorporate the eggs one by one.
5. Add the milk, and sift the dry ingredients into the mixing bowl. Mix well, but take care not to overmix, or your pudding will be stodgy. Pour the batter into the buttered baking dish.
6. Arrange the apple slices on top. Bake for around 45 minutes until the edges are golden. Remove from the oven.

Sauce:

7. Add the butter, sugar, and milk to a small saucepan, and boil for 5 minutes. Remove from heat, and stir in the caramel essence.

FINAL TOUCHES

8. Pour the sauce over the pudding. Serve with ice cream, whipped cream, or make your own egg custard (see page 246).

Post Toasties Tart SERVES 6–8

Post Toasties Tart is another one of my earliest food memories. I can't remember whether I first discovered its deliciousness at my ouma's (grandmother's) house during holidays or at home, but it was love at first bite.

Post Toasties was an early competitor of Kellogg's cornflakes. I think it was introduced in South Africa before cornflakes were, so the name stuck, and the older generations still refer to any type of cornflakes as Post Toasties (often used as one word, *Postoasties*). The creamy, custardy filling with crunchy crust works every time and is bound to stir up some nostalgia among those of us who, shall we say, are more advanced in our years.

EXTRA GEAR

Electric beater

INGREDIENTS

Crust

3 cups cornflakes
½ cup melted butter
½ cup sugar
1 tsp cinnamon

Filling

6 eggs
4 cups full cream milk
4 heaping Tbsp all-purpose flour
½ cup sugar
2 tsp vanilla extract
1 Tbsp butter

PREP

Crust:

1. Crush the cornflakes by pulsing in a food processor or popping them in a plastic bag, pressing the air out, and pounding with a rolling pin.
2. Mix all the ingredients for the crust together, and press it down evenly into the base of the baking dish.

Filling:

3. Separate the eggs (see page 37) with egg yolks in one container and egg whites in another. You'll need both. Warm the milk to just below boiling point in a small pot, or use the microwave.

METHOD

Filling:

4. Mix the flour, sugar, and egg yolks together in a pot. Add a little of the milk, and whisk into a smooth paste. Add the rest of the milk while whisking.
5. Pop the pot on the stove, and bring the mixture to a boil while stirring with a wooden spoon. It will thicken into a smooth custard. Remove from heat, add the vanilla extract and butter, and stir through.
6. Whisk the egg whites with an electric beater until it forms stiff peaks when you lift up the beater.
7. Pour the custard over the crust you prepared earlier, and pop the egg whites on top, smoothing it out with a rubber spatula or spoon.
8. Bake for about 25 minutes until golden brown on top. Remove from the oven, and allow to cool.

Roasted Marrow Bones SERVES 4

My first experience of a proper steakhouse was at Die President Hotel in Riversdale, a slightly bigger town about half an hour's drive from Heidelberg, South Africa, where I grew up. Once a month, our family and friends would go there for dinner, and the kids were told to be on their best behavior (as if).

I don't remember too much about the place, but the one thing I remember clear as day is the delicious roasted marrow bones they served with a slice of toast. It was the best thing I ever tasted.

Fast forward about twenty years, and I read about English chef Fergus Henderson (who founded the restaurant St. John in London) and his nose-to-tail approach to cooking meat. This really resonated with me, as my dad had taught me to eat offal and other "less prized" cuts of meat from an early age. He had grown up in a time where absolutely nothing was wasted.

People raved about Henderson's roasted marrow bones and parsley salad, which reminded me of the marrow bones I had had at Die President Hotel. Even though I had neither Henderson's recipe nor theirs, I was determined to come up with my own, and here is the result.

Marrow bones are extremely rich and fatty. They're definitely not something you want to eat every day, but if you want to treat a carnivore in your life to a good meal, this is the way to do it.

INGREDIENTS

- 4 beef marrow bones, 8 inches long, sawed in half lengthwise (canoe cut)
- ½ cup coarse breadcrumbs
- 1 loaf sourdough bread
- Salt
- Cracked black pepper

Parsley salad

- 1 cup Italian flat leaf parsley
- ½ onion
- 2 cloves garlic
- 2 tsp drained capers
- ½ lemon
- 2 Tbsp extra virgin olive oil, plus extra to drizzle

NOTES:
If you can't find "canoe cut" marrow bones, you can also use the round cut version, which works just as well. I just prefer the canoe cut for presentation and scooping purposes.

PREP

1. Preheat the oven to 400°F / 200°C.

Parsley salad:

2. Roughly chop the Italian parsley, set about 2 tablespoons aside, and add the rest to a bowl. Chop the onion, garlic, and capers finely, and add to the bowl.

3. Zest the lemon with a grater. Add the zest as well as the lemon juice to the bowl. Add the olive oil and a strong pinch of salt and pepper, and mix through.

4. Add the reserved 2 tablespoons of parsley to the breadcrumbs and mix through.

METHOD

5. Lightly scrunch up some aluminum foil, and place on a baking sheet. Arrange the bones cut-side-up, and gently press them down into the foil, so the foil keeps the bones securely in place, as level as possible.

6. Season generously with salt and freshly cracked black pepper, then sprinkle breadcrumbs on top.

7. Roast in the oven for about 20–25 minutes until the breadcrumbs start to turn golden, then turn on the broiler and crisp up the top, about 5 minutes. Remove from the oven and allow to cool slightly.

8. Slice the sourdough bread, drizzle with olive oil, and arrange on a baking sheet. Toast in the oven for about 5 minutes until golden brown. If the bones have cooled down too much by now, reheat them for a few minutes—they need to be served hot.

FINAL TOUCHES

9. Serve with the parsley salad in small bowls along with the toast (and plenty of napkins). Use spoons to scoop out the marrow and spread it on a piece of toast, then top with the parsley salad and a small pinch of salt.

10. Grab a piece of toast and rub it up and down the inside of the bone to get the last bits out. Enjoy, then wipe the smile (and fat) off your face.

My Dad's Oxtail Stew

SERVES 8

If I ever found myself at the wrong end of death row, my dad's oxtail potjie would be my last meal, hands down.

Potjie is an Afrikaans word for the big cast iron pots in which we cook stews low and slow on small wood fires. (We have normal kitchens too, don't worry.) *Potjiekos* (pot food) , pronounced "poy-kee-kos," is a big part of South Africa's cultural heritage, much like the more popular *braai*—grilling (primarily meat) over hot coals.

This is a very simple stew, but its beauty is in that simplicity. My dad is a firm believer of the mantra "less is more" when it comes to cooking (except his portions, which are huge). In the case of oxtail, I agree with him. I've cooked many other versions using wine, lots more vegetables, herbs, and spices, and while some of those are great, this one is still my favorite. Because the added flavors are minimal, you allow the individual ingredients to shine.

Since I understand that not everyone can just go ahead and make a wood fire in their backyard these days, I'll give you the stovetop version below.

EXTRA GEAR

1 really big pot

INGREDIENTS

5 lb oxtail
2 medium yellow onions, peeled
3 Tbsp vegetable oil
Salt
2 Tbsp Worcestershire sauce
3–4 medium potatoes
6 medium carrots
1 Tbsp corn flour
2 tsp dried Italian herbs
1 tsp sweet paprika
Cracked black pepper

PREP

1. Cut the oxtail into 1½-inch chunks. Roughly chop the onions.

2. Bring the pot up to medium-high heat, and add enough vegetable oil to cover the bottom.

3. Fry the oxtail pieces until brown on all sides, about 5–10 minutes. Add the chopped onions to the pot along with enough water to cover the meat by 2 inches. Add 2 tablespoons of salt and the Worcestershire sauce, and bring to a boil.

4. Turn the heat down to a gentle rolling boil, lid the pot, and cook for 3 hours, depending on how tough your meat is. The meat will start pulling away from the bone and feel softer to the touch, but you won't be able to push the meat off the bone yet. That's when you know you're ready for the next step.

METHOD

5. Peel the potatoes, cut them into quarters, and add them to the pot. Peel the carrots, slice them into ½-inch chunks, and add to the pot.

6. Remove the lid, and let it simmer for about 45 minutes or so. The sauce will start thickening as the water cooks out. You need to stir and check the liquid levels every 20 minutes or so.

7. Add a bit of water if things get too dry, but don't add too much—you want to cook off most of the water to end up with a rich, meaty sauce that sticks to the roof of your mouth.

8. In the last 20 minutes or so, mix the corn flour, Italian herbs, and paprika in a cup with some water, and add it to the pot. Stir through.

9. When the meat can be easily pushed off the bone and the vegetables can be easily pierced with a fork, your work here is done.

FINAL TOUCHES

10. Serve this on rice or some crusty bread. Keep it simple.

NOTES:

If you are man enough, go ahead and cook it on a fire. Just manage the heat levels by using small pieces of firewood, and cook it low and slow.

This recipe does take a long time to prepare. Oxtail is one of the toughest cuts of beef around, so we need to soften it by boiling it for a few hours. For the first 3 hours, you can basically leave it alone, while just checking water levels from time to time.

If your sauce is too watery by the time all the ingredients are cooked, fish out the meat and most of the veggies from the pot, and boil the liquid until the water has cooked off enough. Then add everything back in, bring up to temperature, and serve.

Basic Recipes

MUSHROOM SAUCE

INGREDIENTS

1 lb fresh mushrooms
Olive oil, for frying
Knob butter, for frying
Salt
2 cups cream
2 cups milk, plus extra
1 tsp Worcestershire sauce
Cracked black pepper
1 tsp dried thyme
1 Tbsp freshly chopped parsley, plus extra to garnish
1 Tbsp cornstarch

METHOD

1. Slice (or roughly chop) the mushrooms. Divide them into batches small enough to not overcrowd your pan.

2. Pop a wide, heavy-bottomed pan on medium-high heat, and add a splash of olive oil. When the oil heats up, add a knob of butter, a pinch of salt, and a batch of mushrooms, being careful not to overcrowd. Fry for 4 minutes until browned, stirring and shaking the pan halfway through. Remove from pan, and set aside.

3. Repeat until all the mushrooms are browned, then add all cooked mushrooms back to the pan. Add remaining ingredients, except the cornstarch, and bring the heat up to just below boiling, stirring as you go. Turn down the heat to a low simmer, and let the mixture reduce for 10–15 minutes, stirring every 5 minutes or so.

4. Now it's up to you to decide how thick you'd like the sauce to be. To thicken it up, mix the cornstarch with just enough water so you can mix it into a smooth paste. Add that to the sauce, stir through, then let simmer for 5 minutes. To loosen things up, add a splash more of milk, and stir through.

5. Garnish with more chopped parsley.

CHEESE SAUCE

> **NOTE:**
> If you are using cold, leftover white sauce, you will need to bring it back to life and up to temperature. Add the white sauce to a pan on medium-high heat along with a couple of splashes of milk. Whisk the mixture constantly as it heats up. Add a little more milk if it refuses to come together. Keep whisking until smooth and creamy.

INGREDIENTS

1 cup white sauce, hot (see page 21)
½ cup grated mature cheddar or Gruyère cheese
¼ cup grated Parmesan cheese
Milk
Salt
Cracked black pepper
Paprika

METHOD

1. Take your freshly prepared white sauce off the heat, and add all the cheese. Stir the sauce with a wooden spoon as the cheese melts until well combined. Add a little more milk if the sauce feels too thick, and a little more cheese if it feels too runny.

2. You can pop the pan back on a little heat while stirring constantly if the cheese has not melted and incorporated into the sauce.

3. Have a taste, and adjust seasoning with a pinch or two of salt and pepper. Garnish with a pinch of paprika on top.

GARLIC AND OREGANO BALSAMIC REDUCTION

> **NOTE:**
> The fumes that come off the pan as you reduce the vinegar can be quite strong, so do this in a well-ventilated area.

INGREDIENTS

2 cups balsamic vinegar
½ cup brown sugar
10 cloves garlic
½ cup loosely packed fresh oregano leaves

METHOD

1. Add the vinegar to a large, wide pan, and place on medium-low heat. Add the brown sugar, and stir well until dissolved. You'll want to be stirring this mixture throughout the process, as the sugar will easily burn at the bottom of the pan.

2. Crack the garlic cloves open by pressing down on them with the flat part of a blade, then add the cracked cloves to the pan, along with the oregano leaves.

3. Keep this liquid slowly simmering, while stirring frequently. I can't give you exact times, as they will differ depending on your stove and pan, but here's how to check for the correct consistency instead. You want the end product to be thick and syrupy at room temperature; however, that same mixture will be much thinner and runnier while on the stove, so what is a man to do? Drizzle a few drops of the hot liquid onto a dinner plate with a spoon, and allow it to cool. Then check the consistency of the cooled liquid.

4. Once the cooled liquid is thick and sticky, immediately remove the pan from heat, strain the liquid through a sieve, and allow to cool. I like to store mine in little plastic squeeze bottles, so I can easily drizzle black gold over my grilled cheese sandwiches.

HOMEMADE EGG CUSTARD

This is a recipe for a standard egg custard, the way your grandma used to make it. It is delicious as is over puddings and desserts, but it can also be used as the base for making homemade ice cream (see page 217).

INGREDIENTS

2 vanilla beans (or 3–4 tsp good-quality vanilla extract)
1 cup full cream milk
3 cups cream (heavy cream, if you dare)
6 egg yolks, separated (see page 37)
¾ cup sugar
1 tsp salt

METHOD

1. If you are using real vanilla beans (good on you), split the beans in half lengthways with a paring knife, and scrape out the seeds with the back of the knife. Add the seeds as well as the husks into the cream.

2. Heat the milk, cream, and vanilla in a pot over medium heat, but do not allow the mixture to boil. If you are using vanilla beans, fish out the husks with a wooden spoon; they've done their part.

3. Whisk the egg yolks, sugar, and salt together in a mixing bowl. Slowly add the hot cream mixture to the eggs, whisking as you go. Return the combined mixture to the pot, and cook over medium-low heat, stirring constantly with a wooden spoon.

4. After about 5–10 minutes, the mixture will thicken slightly and coat the back of the spoon. Do not overheat this mixture—if you see "curds" resembling scrambled eggs forming, your heat is too high or you are not stirring enough. Remove from heat, and stir vigorously. Pass the mixture through a fine wire sieve to remove some of those curds (if they do form) when you pour the custard into a serving jug.

HOMEMADE MELBA TOAST

INGREDIENTS

1 French baguette or similar white bread, a day or two old

METHOD

1. Preheat the oven to 300°F / 150°C.

2. Slice the bread as thinly as you safely can. Bread that is a day or two old will have firmed up quite a bit, making it easier to slice thinly. Take your time with this.

3. Arrange the slices on a baking sheet, and bake for about 5–6 minutes until it just starts to brown. Gently turn the slices over, and bake for another 5 minutes.

4. The bread should be light in color and crispy to the touch. Remove from the baking sheet, and allow to cool on a cooling rack.

HOMEMADE BREADCRUMBS

INGREDIENTS

Couple of slices of whatever bread you have lying around that is about to go stale (I like to use baguette or ciabatta)

METHOD

1. Preheat the oven to 300°F / 150°C.

2. Cut the bread into roughly 1-inch cubes, lay out on a baking sheet, and pop in the oven. After 10 minutes, flip the chunks over, and let them bake for another 10 minutes.

3. Remove from the oven, and allow to cool. Once cool, add them to a mortar and pestle, and begin crushing. How fine you go is up to you, but I like to leave them fairly chunky. You can always grind them down a little more later.

4. If you do not have a mortar and pestle, wait for the chunks of bread to cool, pop them in a plastic bag, squeeze out most of the air, then crush the bread with a rolling pin.

5. Store in an airtight container.

BASIC BREAD DOUGH

INGREDIENTS

1½ cups lukewarm water, plus extra
1½ cups milk
2 Tbsp melted butter
2 tsp sugar
2 tsp instant yeast
5 cups flour
1 tsp salt

METHOD

1. Add the water, milk, butter, sugar, and yeast to a mixing jug. Stir, and set aside.

2. Add the flour and salt to a large mixing bowl, and mix through with your fingers. Make a well in the middle of the flour, and pour in the wet ingredients. Combine the ingredients with a wooden spoon.

3. Using your hands, knead the mixture for 5 minutes to form a smooth and elastic ball of dough. If the dough is sticky, it is too wet—add a little flour, and keep kneading until you get a smooth surface.

4. Pop the dough into a large mixing bowl, and set aside, covered, to rest for about an hour until doubled in size.

5. Punch down the dough with your fists, then knead for 3 minutes or more, and let rest covered for another 30 minutes or so. The dough is now ready for use, either for baking bread or as a general-purpose dough for baked goodies. Try it with Tomato & Feta Pull-Apart Rolls (see page 175).

HERBED PAPRIKA SALT

INGREDIENTS

2 Tbsp kosher salt
1 tsp paprika
1 tsp dried oregano
1 tsp dried thyme
1 tsp dried chives

METHOD

1. Mix all the ingredients together with a fork, then store in an airtight container.

TOMATO SALT

INGREDIENTS

2 lb cherry or plum tomatoes
2 cups (about 1 lb) flaky sea salt (like Maldon)

METHOD

1. Preheat the oven to 250°F / 120°.

2. Slice the tomatoes in half, and pop them on a baking sheet (or two), cut side up. Sprinkle some salt over the top, then pop the baking sheet in the oven.

3. Slowly roast the tomatoes for 4–6 hours, depending on the size of tomatoes used. You want them to shrink and be dried on the edges, but still have a little juice on the inside. Remove the tomatoes from the oven, and allow to cool.

4. Chop the tomatoes as fine as you can with a chef's knife, or blitz them in a food processor. Mix the chopped tomatoes with the rest of the salt, and stir through.

5. The mixture should be a bit wet at this stage. Transfer to another baking sheet, and roast in the oven again, about an hour or so. Check that the salt mixture is dry, and break up any remaining clumps. Allow to cool completely, then store in airtight containers.

BASIL SALT

INGREDIENTS

2 cups (about 1 lb) flaky sea salt (like Maldon)
1 cup (tightly packed) fresh basil leaves

METHOD

1. Preheat the oven to 212°F / 100°C.

2. Wash the basil leaves under cool running water, then pick off the stems if they are very woody and hard.

3. On a large cutting board, roughly chop the leaves up with a chef's knife, then add 1 cup of salt and mix it all through with your hands.

4. Chop the mixture up some more until the basil is nice and fine, then add and mix through the other cup of salt. You'll see the salt soak up all the juices that the basil released during chopping. The mixture should be slightly wet at this point.

5. Spread the mixture out evenly on a baking tray, then bake at 212°F / 100°C for about an hour, stirring and breaking up any clumps that form every 15 minutes.

6. Once the mixture is completely dry, remove from the oven, and allow to cool. Break up any remaining clumps, and store in airtight containers.

Cooking Terms

AL DENTE

Literally translated as *to the tooth,* it refers to a stage of cooking where an ingredient is cooked, but still offers a little resistance in the center when you bite into it.

BAKING

To cook an ingredient using dry heat, usually in an oven.

BASTING

To pour or brush fat, juices, sauce, or marinade over the surface of an ingredient during cooking to prevent it from drying out and improve flavor. Generally used when roasting or grilling meats.

BEATING

To rapidly stir a mixture until smooth and combined using a spoon, fork, whisk, or electric mixer.

BLANCHING

To briefly cook an ingredient by dropping it in boiling water for a short period of time. Usually followed by "shocking," which means to drop an ingredient in ice water to cool it down rapidly and stop the cooking process.

BOUQUET GARNI (OR FLAVOR BOMB)

The French term for a bundle of herbs usually tied together with string and added to soups, stocks, and stews to add flavor. The bundle is cooked with the rest of the ingredients and then easily removed at a later stage.

BRAISING

A combination cooking method where large cuts of meat are first seared at high heat and then cooked in a covered pot at lower heat in a small amount of liquid.

BROILING

Similar to grilling, where an ingredient is cooked by intense, direct heat. Home ovens generally have a broiler element in its roof for this purpose.

CHIFFONADE

A knife technique where herbs or leafy greens are rolled up and then sliced into very thin ribbons.

COMPOTE

Fresh or dried fruit (whole or cut into pieces) slowly cooked into a sugar syrup, often containing wine or liquor and spices.

COULIS

A thick, smooth sauce made from fruit or vegetables that are cooked, pureed, and then strained.

CREAMING

The process of combining several ingredients (typically butter and sugar) by whipping them together to form a smooth, aerated paste. A wooden spoon can be used, but an electric beater or stand mixer makes things much easier.

CRIMPING

The process of sealing the top and bottom layers of pastry together by pressing them together into small regular folds, often using a fork or special crimping tool.

DEEP-FRYING

To fry food in enough hot oil that covers it completely.

DEGLAZING

The process of removing small browned bits of food residue from the bottom of the pan and dissolving it in a liquid to form a *fond* (French for *foundation*). The fond is then used as the base for sauces, soups, or gravies.

DICING

A knife technique where the ingredient is cut into small blocks (or dice) of a specific size. You'll hear people talk of a small or medium dice.

DREDGING

The process of coating a wet ingredient with a dry one. Think chicken breasts and flour. The wet ingredient is rolled or pulled through the dry ingredient until an event coating is achieved.

DRIZZLING

The process of pouring a thin stream of liquid over other ingredients in a random pattern.

DUSTING

The process of sprinkling a fine layer of powdered or granulated ingredient over another ingredient or a surface. For example, a cake may be dusted with cocoa powder as a garnish, or a work surface can be dusted with flour prior to working dough on it.

FOLDING

The process of gently combining two mixtures (one often aerated) with each other without getting rid of the air bubbles trapped in one or both mixtures.

FOND

A liquid containing the highly flavorful small browned bits of food residue left in a pan after frying meats or vegetables. This liquid is created by the deglazing process and used as the base for sauces, soups, or gravies.

FRYING

To cook food in a small amount of fat or oil, typically in a pan.

GLAZING

A glaze is a glossy coating applied to foods. It can be sweet or savory. For example, a chocolate glaze can be poured over a cake, or a glaze can be formed on a roast by basting it with the pan juices or other sauces during cooking.

GREASING

The process of coating the inside of a baking vessel with butter or fat to prevent sticking.

GRILL

A cooking technique where dry heat, often at high temperatures, are applied to the surface of the food from above or below.

JULIENNE

A knife technique where vegetables are cut into thin, matchstick-like pieces.

KNEADING

To work a piece of dough by pressing it down with the palm of your hand while stretching it out forward. You then fold it over, turn it a quarter turn to the side, and repeat. This is done to properly combine all the ingredients as well as to develop gluten structure (where applicable).

LEAVENING

Leavening, or raising agents, are a number of different ingredients used in doughs and batters to create air bubbles. These small air bubbles expand during cooking, which makes the dough rise in height and become lighter and softer in the process. Examples are baking powder in cakes and yeast in breads.

MINCING

A knife technique where the ingredient is broken down into very small pieces, much smaller than you'll be able to achieve by chopping or dicing.

MIREPOIX (FRENCH)

A flavor base of onions, carrots, and celery that are sautéed in butter or oil. This is the starting point for many, many soups, stews, and sauces. It is also often used as a bed for a roast to lay on, and then turned into a sauce of gravy at the end.

MISE EN PLACE

A French term meaning "set in place" or "everything in its place." The idea is to have all the ingredients needed to cook a dish prepped and ready to go, often in a number of small containers.

POACHING

A cooking technique where the ingredient is submerged and cooked in a liquid at a relatively low temperature, usually between 140°F / 60°C and 180°F / 80°C.

POMME PURÉE

Basically a fancy way of saying mashed potatoes. A good pomme purée will be very smooth and silky, while mashed potatoes generally describe a chunkier affair.

PROOFING (OR PROVING)

The process of allowing a dough to rise due to yeast action for a period of time.

PUREE

A thick liquid of crushed or liquidized ingredients, usually fruits or vegetables. Ingredients can either be processed in a blender, or crushed and pushed through a sieve.

RAGÙ

A thick meat sauce made with various kinds of minced or chopped meat and vegetables, generally served with pasta. Think cannelloni (see page 101).

REDUCING

The process of simmering or boiling a liquid for an extended period of time to remove water and concentrate the flavor. As water cooks out, the liquid will also change in consistency, becoming thicker the longer you cook it.

RESTING

The process of allowing a piece of meat to "rest" at room temperature for a period of time after cooking. This is believed to cause the meat to retain more of its juices once you slice into it.

ROASTING

A cooking technique where dry and relatively high heat (300°F / 150°C and higher) is applied to an ingredient in a way where the heat envelops the food and cooks it from all sides. Typically done in an oven.

ROUX

A paste used as thickening agent. It is made by adding equal amounts (by weight) of flour and fat (typically butter) to a pan, mixing them together into a paste, and cooking it for a few minutes to get rid of the "raw flour" taste.

SAUTÉ

The process of frying foods on high heat in a small amount of fat. The word *sauté* is translated as *bounce* or *jump*, in reference to the way cooks often toss the contents of a pan with short, quick wrist movements. If you are not that skilled, simply move things around constantly with a wooden spoon to prevent burning and achieve even browning.

SCALDING

Scalding can mean many things depending on the context. In cooking, it is generally used when referring to milk, and it means heating up the milk to just below boiling point, when small bubbles start forming around the edges of the pan.

SCORING

The process of cutting small lines across the surface of an ingredient. Sometimes done to increase flavor by allowing seasoning to get "inside" the food, it also helps prevent meat from curling up during cooking.

SEARING

The process of browning the surface of food by exposing it to very high heat for a short amount of time until a caramelized crust forms.

SHALLOW FRYING

The process of cooking food in a small amount of preheated fat or oil. The oil should be deep enough to go about halfway up the ingredient being cooked.

SHOCKING

To drop an ingredient in ice water to cool it down rapidly and stop the cooking process. Usually done after "blanching."

SIMMERING

To gently cook food in a liquid that is kept just below the boiling point of water. Small amounts of bubble appear here and there, but the liquid is not at a full boil.

SKIMMING

To remove a layer of foam or fat from a liquid by scooping it off with a spoon (slotted spoon for foam, normal spoon or ladle for fat).

STRAINING

To pour a mixture of liquid and solids through a sieve or strainer to separate the solids from the liquid.

SMOKING POINT

The temperature at which an oil or fat starts to burn and release smoke. High smoking point oils are better suited for high-temperature cooking.

SWEATING

The process of cooking food (like onions) in a small amount of fat on medium-low heat to release moisture and soften the cell walls. The intention is not to brown the food but to cook until soft and translucent. Sometimes a little liquid is added and the pan is covered with a lid to prevent browning.

TOP AND TAIL

When prepping vegetables, to "top and tail" means cutting a slice off each end and discarding it.

UMAMI

The so-called "fifth" taste after salty, sweet, bitter, and sour. It was discovered in the early 1900s by a Japanese chemistry professor named Kikunae Ikeda. There is no English word to describe it adequately but it is often described as a "meaty" or "savory" taste.

Index

Conversion Charts

METRIC AND IMPERIAL CONVERSIONS

(THESE CONVERSIONS ARE ROUNDED FOR CONVENIENCE)

Ingredient	Cups/Tablespoons/ Teaspoons	Ounces	Grams/Milliliters
Butter	1 cup/ 16 tablespoons/ 2 sticks	8 ounces	230 grams
Cheese, shredded	1 cup	4 ounces	110 grams
Cream cheese	1 tablespoon	0.5 ounce	14.5 grams
Cornstarch	1 tablespoon	0.3 ounce	8 grams
Flour, all-purpose	1 cup/1 tablespoon	4.5 ounces/0.3 ounce	125 grams/8 grams
Flour, whole wheat	1 cup	4 ounces	120 grams
Fruit, dried	1 cup	4 ounces	120 grams
Fruits or veggies, chopped	1 cup	5 to 7 ounces	145 to 200 grams
Fruits or veggies, puréed	1 cup	8.5 ounces	245 grams
Honey, maple syrup, or corn syrup	1 tablespoon	.75 ounce	20 grams
Liquids: cream, milk, water, or juice	1 cup	8 fluid ounces	240 milliliters
Oats	1 cup	5.5 ounces	150 grams
Salt	1 teaspoon	0.2 ounce	6 grams
Spices: cinnamon, cloves, ginger, or nutmeg (ground)	1 teaspoon	0.2 ounce	5 milliliters
Sugar, brown, firmly packed	1 cup	7 ounces	200 grams
Sugar, white	1 cup/1 tablespoon	7 ounces/0.5 ounce	200 grams/12.5 grams
Vanilla extract	1 teaspoon	0.2 ounce	4 grams

OVEN TEMPERATURES

Fahrenheit	Celsius	Gas Mark
225°	110°	¼
250°	120°	½
275°	140°	1
300°	150°	2
325°	160°	3
350°	180°	4
375°	190°	5
400°	200°	6
425°	220°	7
450°	230°	8